Mag. Claudia Lichtenwagner

SMILE 4
Grammar

Englisch Übungsbuch für die
4. Klasse Mittelschule / AHS

Von Claudia Lichtenwagner bisher im G&G Verlag erschienen:

Smile Listening Comprehensions 1 (978-3-7074-1978-8)
Smile Listening Comprehensions 2 (978-3-7074-2061-6)
Smile Listening Comprehensions 3 (978-3-7074-2184-2)
Smile Listening Comprehensions 4 (978-3-7074-2187-3)

Smile 1 Grammar (978-3-7074-1306-9)
Smile 2 Grammar (978-3-7074-1307-6)
Smile 3 Grammar (978-3-7074-1308-3)
Smile 4 Grammar (978-3-7074-1309-0)

Smile Reading Comprehensions 1 (978-3-7074-1354-0)
Smile Reading Comprehensions 2 (978-3-7074-1508-7)
Smile Reading Comprehensions 3 (978-3-7074-1624-4)
Smile Reading Comprehensions 4 (978-3-7074-1846-0)

Smile Matura-Trainer Speaking Competences (978-3-7074-2080-7)

Sourire 1 (978-3-7074-1310-6)
Sourire 2 (978-3-7074-1311-3)
Sourire 3 (978-3-7074-1312-0)
Sourire 4 (978-3-7074-1313-7)
Sourire 5 (978-3-7074-1314-4)

 Dieses Werk ist für den Schul- und Unterrichtsgebrauch bestimmt.

Es darf gemäß § 42 (3) des Urheberrechtsgesetzes auch für den eigenen Unterrichtsgebrauch nicht vervielfältigt werden.

SMILE – die erfolgreichste Englisch-Lernhilfenreihe
jetzt auch online auf

- Über 6.500 interaktive Übungen zu allen Grammatik-Themen
- Wiederholung, Testvorbereitung und Hausaufgaben mit automatisierten Auswertungen zur Selbstüberprüfung
- https://eduactive.at/smile-englisch-grammatik-4-e-learning.html

www.ggverlag.at

ISBN 978-3-7074-1309-0

30. Auflage 2025

Druck und Bindung: Brüder Glöckler, Wöllersdorf

© 2010 G&G Verlagsgesellschaft mbH, Frankgasse 4, 1090 Wien
produktsicherheit@ggverlag.at
Alle Rechte vorbehalten. Jede Art der Vervielfältigung, auch die des auszugsweisen Nachdrucks, der fotomechanischen Wiedergabe, der Einspeicherung und Verarbeitung in elektronische Systeme sowie Text- und Data-Mining sind ohne ausdrückliche Zustimmung des Verlages gesetzlich verboten.
Gedruckt auf Papier aus geprüfter nachhaltiger Forstwirtschaft.

VORWORT

Liebe Schülerin, lieber Schüler!

Der vierte Band der SMILE-Serie behandelt wichtige Grammatikkapitel aus dem 4. Lernjahr. Wie immer folgen zahlreiche Übungen auf die übersichtlich zusammengestellten Grammatikregeln.
Im Anschluss daran findest du Vokabelerklärungen und einen äußerst genauen "Key" mit Seitenangaben, wo du die passende Regel, die im jeweiligen Fall zur Anwendung kommt, nachlesen kannst.
SMILE Grammar I, II und III solltest du griffbereit zur Hand haben, um wichtige Kapitel nachlesen zu können, auf denen der 4. Band aufbaut.

Ich wünsche dir großen Erfolg beim Lernen!

Prof. Mag. Claudia Lichtenwagner

CONTENTS

	page
Revision: Comparison of adjectives	1
Revision: *Some, any*	2
Revision: Passive	3
Revision: Adjective or adverb	4
Phrasal verbs	5
Modal verbs	9
Revision: Will- or going to-future	10
Revision: Past perfect tense simple	10
Reporting verbs	11
Reported questions	12
Reported commands	16
Reported exclamations	20
Reported speech: Special cases	21
Say or *tell*	23
How to translate „*lassen*"	28
Infinitive with to	35
Infinitive without to	40
Infinitive shortens sentences	43
Object with the infinitive with to	46
Object with the infinitive without to	47
Passive infinitive	53
How to translate German „*man*"	58
Perfect infinitive	61
Continuous infinitive	61
Gerund	63
I used to or *I'm used to*	84
Gerund shortens sentences	86
Revision: Conditional	89
Revision: Contact clauses	89
Past perfect tense progressive	90
Participle	91
Words	95
Key	98

COMPARISON OF ADJECTIVES

First revise ☺ II pages 33–44

1. Dad's new car is much .... (fast) than the old one. Dad says it is even twice as .... (fast) as our previous car and it is much .... (comfortable). Even its colour is .... (nice). But, unfortunately, it was far .... (expensive).
2. The Picture of Dorian Gray is the .... (exciting) film I've ever seen.
3. Isn't it .... (marvellous) to lie in the warm sand?
4. Last winter was .... (rough) than the winter before and this summer is .... (hot and dry) than last summer.
5. Paris is the .... (marvellous) city I've ever visited.
6. I find scuba diving .... (fascinating) than climbing.
7. What the Aborigines need is .... (good) education and .... (good) health care.
8. A trip to Florida is the .... (good) holiday I can imagine.
9. This is the .... (bad) thunderstorm I've ever experienced.
10. In former days punishment was .... (severe) than nowadays, grandfather always says.
11. His visit was extremely .... (unpleasant). He always thinks he is the .... (good), ... (handsome) and .... (clever) guy in the world.
12. She always wears the .... (late) fashion. All her things are .... (brand-new).
13. His thirst grew .... (strong) and .... (strong).
14. Sydney's opera house is the .... (spectacular) building I've ever seen.
15. Sarah says that the .... (great) place for a holiday is at home because it is .... (relaxing) than being in the heat somewhere.
16. For Paul wasps are .... (dangerous) than bees because he is allergic to them.
17. Please could you take me to the .... (near) hospital?
18. You should eat .... (few) crisps. They are not as .... (healthy) as apples or cereals.
19. For me, to be a flying doctor would be the .... (interesting) job.
20. My .... (near) car will be a .... (big) one.
21. Yesterday there were .... (few) people at the concert than .... (late) time. I think the weather was too .... (beautiful).
22. He found this test .... (difficult) than the .... (late).

SOME ANY

First revise ☺ II pages 18–23, ☺ III page 19

1. He'd love to find .... he really loves.
2. Please think of .... to help her.
3. I can't understand how .... likes watching boxing.
4. I'm awfully sorry, but I couldn't do ....
5. Isn't there .... note for me?
   I'm waiting for .... important messages.
6. Would you like .... to nibble? .... peanuts, or perhaps .... crisps?
7. He always attracts pupils ....
8. Haven't you got .... news of Mr Smith from the hospital?
   They say that he has .... tropical disease.
9. I bet he hasn't got .... plan for what he should do after school.
10. Do you practise .... regular sport?
11. I found this pink and black stone .... near the river.
12. He wants to develop .... self-discipline by practising sport.
13. She lives in .... village high up the mountain.
14. I feel a terrible pain .... in my stomach.
15. Please tell me, are there .... positive aspects of extreme sports?
    I can't imagine ....!
16. He didn't have .... good experiences when he went on a hiking tour all alone.
17. Please turn down the radio. I can't stand .... noise now.
18. Have you seen my racket .... ?
    It must be .... in the cellar.
19. Which dress shall I buy? – .... of them! They are both very chic.
20. There was .... noise .... in the garden. – Really?
    I didn't hear ....
21. Grandpa invented .... strange machine for stirring dough.
22. .... madness drove him up the steep rock face.
23. Paula tries .... miracle drug she can get.
24. Oh no, ... has knocked over my glass of wine!
25. There's an article about her .... in the local paper.
26. .... coffee, Tim? – No, thanks I wouldn't like .... just now.
27. He was desperate because .... had stolen his bike.
28. I saw .... interesting on TV yesterday.
29. Finally she managed to pass all her exams ....
30. If .... wants to talk to Dr Roberts, please call now.
31. She refused to tell .... her secret.

PASSIVE

Fill in the appropriate passive forms. Mind the tenses!
First revise ☺ III pages 89–93.

1. Mrs Miller's purse .... (steal) when she was on her way home. The thief .... (arrest) shortly after.
2. Tom's bike .... (repair) when father comes home in the evening.
3. I'm sure that my room .... (paint) during the next holidays.
4. When mum came home from work all the dishes .... (wash).
5. Have you bought all the food that .... (need) for cooking now?
6. If he goes on being lazy like this he .... (dismiss).
7. Chris is a perfect tennis player. He .... (not / beat) up to now.
8. Thousands of Indians .... (drive away) from their country and most of them .... (kill) during their fight for their lands. The others .... (place) on reservations.
9. He .... (see) as one of the most important experts on culture.
10. The Rockefeller Center .... (name) after J. D. Rockefeller Jr. and the first buildings .... (build) between 1931 and 1940.
11. These shirts .... (make) in China.
12. Taste this sweet. It .... (make) of marzipan.
13. Thomas .... (call) "Thomas Tomato" by everybody.
14. John F. Kennedy .... (assassinate) in 1963.
15. This delicious cake .... (bake) by mum.
16. The boys ran off after the window .... (shoot in).
17. The bridge .... (repair) for more than twelve weeks during the last holidays.
18. The road .... (tar) at the moment. It .... (not / can / use) now.
19. I thought their house .... (sell).
20. Your homework .... (must / do) carefully.
21. Do you think we .... (may / invite)?
22. The children .... (ought to / give) some extra pocket money for helping so much.
23. There's a good film on. It .... (produce) by Stephen Spielberg.

ADJECTIVE OR ADVERB

Revise ☺ III pages 34–53 first.

1. Tomato soup tastes .... (good).
2. Mr Miller speaks .... (extreme, slow).
3. Did they win the match? – No, they played .... (pretty, bad).
4. She is always .... (friendly) to her pupils.
5. Tom stopped .... (short) when he saw a mouse in the grass.
6. When she shouted at me I was .... (deep) hurt.
7. Ten people had to live in an .... (extreme, small) tent in the refugee camp.
8. She types quite .... (fast) on the computer.
9. Turn off that music, it sounds .... (horrible).
10. Father suggested spending our holidays in Ireland and we all .... (ready) agreed.
11. I was .... (real, high) astonished at her behaving so .... (bad).
12. Nora .... (close) resembles her grandmother.
13. Mum looked for her purse .... (nervous).
14. She grew very .... (angry) when she found that her bike had been stolen.
15. She looks .... (pretty) in her new dress. – Yes, she's always .... (pretty) dressed.
16. It is getting .... (dark). Let's light a candle.
17. The train goes .... (direct) to London. So you needn't change.
18. He climbed .... (quick) out of the car because there was smoke all over.
19. Linda thinks that Campari tastes .... (awful, bitter).
20. We receive letters from Jane .... (monthly).
21. He cannot accept bad marks .... (easy).
22. Too much salt is .... (high, dangerous) for your heart.
23. Your birthday is in May if I remember .... (right).
24. He tasted the Coke .... (careful) to see if there was any alcohol in it.
25. He had to pay .... (dear) for his success.
26. My new silk pyjamas feel .... (soft).
27. The young dog is jumping around .... (lively).
28. Phil looks after his little brother .... (careful).
29. We haven't seen Joe .... (late).
30. Please don't play me .... (false).
31. He was .... (severe) hurt in an accident. He still doesn't feel well.

PHRASAL VERBS

Revise ☺ II pp 58–61 first.

get	bekommen, werden
get **about**	herumkommen
get **across**	hinüber/herüberkommen; klarmachen (idea)
get **ahead / on**	vorankommen
get **along**	zurechtkommen
get **away**	entkommen
get **away with**	mit etwas davonkommen
get **over**	hinüber/herübergehen; über etwas hinwegkommen
get **back**	zurückbekommen; wieder nach Hause kommen
get **out of**	herauskommen
get **off**	aussteigen
get **round**	herumkriegen; etwas vermeiden
get **through**	durchkommen (Telefon); schaffen
get **up**	aufstehen

He can't **get about** like he used to because he's too ill to travel.
We **got across** the bridge.
How are you **getting ahead / on / along** with your work?
He **gets along** well without any help.
The thieves **got away**.
She is bad but she always **gets away with** it.
They **got over** to the other side.
She can't **get over** his death.
When will we **get back**?
I don't think I'll ever **get** my money **back** again.
She managed to **get out of** the burning house.
We **got off** at King's Road.
He always **gets** the girls **round** somehow.
She always tries to **get round** her problems by telling lies.
All the lines were engaged, we couldn't **get through**.
She **got through** her exams.
I like to **get up** early in the morning.

| long **for** | sich sehnen |

I am **longing for** a cool drink now.

hurry	sich beeilen
hurry **up**	sich beeilen
hurry **along**	entlangeilen
hurry **away / off**	wegeilen
hurry **on**	weitereilen, weitermachen
hurry **into**	hineintreiben

Hurry up, we are late!
The man **hurried along** the road.
They **hurried along** the wall.
After they had stolen the pears they **hurried away / off**.
She **hurried on** to say that she was pleased to be with us.
Don't **hurry** me **into** a decision.

hang	hängen
hang **about / around**	herumhängen
hang **on to**	behalten, sich klammern
hang **on**	warten; am Apparat bleiben
hang **up**	aufhängen (Telefon)

I can't stand people **hanging around / about** doing nothing.
She **hangs on to** her old coat.
Please **hang on** for a moment! Don't **hang up**!

drive	fahren
drive **off / away**	wegfahren; vertreiben
drive **in / into**	hineinfahren; hineintreiben (Nagel)
drive **at**	auf etwas hinauswollen

Father **drove off** at seven.
The police **drove** the people **off**.
Please **drive into** the garage because I can't drive **in**.
Father **drove** the nail **in**.
I don't see what you're **driving at**.

sort	sortieren
sort **out**	aussortieren, in Ordnung bringen
sort **through**	durchsehen, aussortieren

Let's **sort out** all our problems.
I'm **sorting through** my old clothes.

fix	befestigen
fix **up**	ausmachen, arrangieren
fix **down / on / to**	befestigen

Let's **fix up** the hotel.
They **fixed up** at time to meet.
Please **fix up** an interview with him.
Could you **fix** this badge **on** my shirt, please?
She always **fixes** her thoughts **on** him.
The shelf is **fixed to** the wall.

carry	tragen
carry **on**	etwas weitertun
carry **off**	hinaustragen, wegtragen
carry **out**	ausführen (Befehle, Aufgaben), hinaustragen

Please help me. I can't **carry on**.
Let's **carry off** the chairs.
The soldiers have to **carry out** orders.

check	nachsehen, fragen
check **up**	überprüfen
check **in**	einchecken

Let's **check (up)** all the addresses.
Where do we have to **check in**? – Gate number three.

put	setzen, stellen, legen
put **up with**	sich abfinden mit
put **up**	anheben; bauen
put **down**	niederschreiben
put **off**	verschieben
put **on**	anziehen
put somebody **up**	jemanden beherbergen

She can't **put up with** his behaviour.
Prices for fuel were **put up**.
They **put up** the building in one year.
I must **put down** his address first.
Never **put off** till tomorrow what you can do today.
Which dress should I **put on**?
You needn't drive home tonight. We'll **put** you **up**.

PHRASAL VERBS

1. Have you fixed .... your trip to London?
2. Did you put .... his telephone number?
3. He put flowers in front of her door and hurried ....
4. We put .... a little shed near the pond.
5. Do they still quarrel? – No, they have sorted it ....
6. He had to put .... his journey because of his illness.
7. Next week I'm going to sort .... all my old photos.
8. The price for bread was put ....
9. Whenever I go to Vienna, Linda puts me ....
10. She gets .... as she did when she was young.
11. The thieves hurried .... Park Road.
12. Hang .... the rope! I'll pull you up!
13. Please fix this button .... my coat, mum.
14. How long will you carry .... tonight? – Till midnight.
15. What are you going to put .... at Frank's party?
16. Unfortunately she drove .... the car in front of her.
17. Please hurry things .... a little.
18. This time he won't get .... it!
19. Don't hang .... please. He is coming.
20. Please carry .... the dustbin.
21. He should put .... the fact that he isn't twenty any more.
22. If we fix this shelf .... the wall, there will be enough place for my books.
23. He carried .... all the instructions, but it didn't work.
24. Where must I get .... ? – King's Park.
25. Michael hangs .... his old things.
26. She must carry .... taking her pills.
27. He can't put .... her constant complaining.
28. She fixed .... a meeting with him.
29. Did she get .... her final exam?
30. I'm longing .... a quiet holiday now.
31. Let me think carefully. You mustn't hurry me .... a decision.
32. This hotel was put .... within three years.
33. Could you hang .... for a few minutes, please?
34. Let's check .... the lists first.
35. When did you fix .... the date?
36. Please put .... what we need for lunch.
37. The policeman is driving the beggar ....
38. I'm afraid we must put .... the meeting.
39. We must check .... at half past nine.
40. You're fixing your eyes .... me! What are you driving
    .... ?

MODAL VERBS + HAVE + PAST PARTICIPLE

Revise ☺ **III** pages 20–21 first.

> These constructions are used to express what in **past** situations **may possibly have happened.**
> *(Diese Konstruktionen werden verwendet, um auszudrücken, was in vergangenen Situationen möglicherweise geschehen hätte können.)*

Examples:

I *could* **have picked** him up.	*Ich hätte ihn abholen können.*
I *may* **have helped** him. =	*Ich hätte ihm vielleicht helfen können.*
I *might* **have helped** him.	

> These constructions are used to express what somebody **should have done** in **past** situations.
> *(Diese Konstruktionen werden verwendet, um auszudrücken, was jemand in vergangenen Situationen hätte tun sollen.)*

Examples:

I *should* **have told** him the truth.	*Ich hätte ihm die Wahrheit sagen sollen.*
I *ought to* **have informed** him.	*Ich hätte ihn eigentlich informieren sollen.*

Fill in: *In the evening Lucy thinks about her day:*

1. I .... (should / do) my homework.
2. I .... (should / help) mum with the cooking.
3. I .... (ought to / phone) Mrs Roberts.
4. I .... (should / prepare) for my Maths test.
5. I .... (should / visit) granny.
6. I .... (ought to / pay) Linda's money back.
7. Peter .... (could / be) nicer to me.
8. Nancy .... (could / take) me to the bus stop but she .... (mightn't / see) me.
9. John's party .... (may / be) great fun.
10. Phil .... (may / be) at John's party.
11. I .... (may / find) the boy of my dreams but he .... (might / dance) with Nelly.
12. Robert .... (ought to / give) me his record.
13. I .... (oughtn't to / tell) Ann about Peter.
14. She .... (may / be) jealous.
15. Peter .... (oughtn't to / kiss) Sarah.

WILL-FUTURE OR GOING TO-FUTURE

Revise ☺ II pages 45–51 first.

1. Mark expects that our planet .... (be) saved.
2. I promise I .... (work) harder next year.
3. We .... (collect) empty bottles and sell them.
4. Frank .... (plant) roses in October.
5. If we harm our environment, we .... (destroy) our planet.
6. I know that he .... (win) the match.
7. I'm afraid you .... (not / be) successful if you don't try harder.
8. We .... (organize) a project on developing countries at school.
9. We .... (possibly start) a cleanup in our hometown.
10. What would you like to eat? – I .... (order) some salad.
11. They .... (buy) a small greenhouse for their garden.
12. When he's eighteen he .... (go) to university.
13. I .... (explain) to you how the machine you bought yesterday works.
14. Wait a moment, I .... (explain) it to you in a minute.
15. I'm certain that he .... (marry) her some day.

PAST PERFECT TENSE SIMPLE

Revise ☺ III pages 60–64 first.

1. I .... (already leave) the house when he came to see me.
2. After he .... (eat) his lunch he felt terribly sick.
3. She .... (just / manage) to close the window when the storm began.
4. After he .... (take) her out to dinner she fell madly in love with him.
5. When Simon was walking in the park he saw that a young lady .... (lose) one glove.
6. After he .... (run) after her to give her the glove she invited him for a cup of coffee.
7. As he .... (forget) to get out of the bus, he had to walk back a long way.
8. After she .... (give) him a kiss both of them went red in the face.
9. He .... (hoover) the carpets before the guests arrived.

REPORTING VERBS

Improve your style: Do not only use **say** or **tell**
(see ☺ **IV** p 23f, GERUND p 63f).

add	*hinzufügen*
admire	*bewundern*
admit, confess	*zugeben*
advise	*raten*
agree	*zustimmen*
ask	*fragen, bitten*
claim	*behaupten, fordern, verlangen*
complain	*sich beklagen*
consider	*betrachten, finden*
continue	*fortfahren, weitersprechen*
deny	*leugnen*
enquire / inquire	*fragen*
expect	*erwarten*
explain / point out	*erklären*
hope	*hoffen*
insist on	*darauf bestehen*
know	*wissen, kennen*
note / mention	*bemerken, erwähnen*
observe	*bemerken, äußern, sagen*
order	*befehlen*
promise	*versprechen*
protest	*protestieren*
refuse	*sich weigern, ablehnen*
regret	*bedauern*
remark	*bemerken*
reply	*erwidern*
suggest that or -ing form	*vorschlagen*
suppose	*vermuten*
think	*glauben, meinen, denken*
to be afraid	*befürchten*
to be amazed, to be astonished	*erstaunt sein*
to be conscious of	*sich bewusst sein*
to be impressed	*beeindruckt sein*
to be indifferent	*gleichgültig sein*
to be interested in	*interessiert sein*
to be sure	*sicher sein*
urge	*drängen, darauf dringen*
want to know / wonder / to be curious to know	*wissen wollen*

REPORTED SPEECH: QUESTIONS

See ☺ III p 69–77 first!

1. with question words:	**when, where, why, how long, how much, who, which, what ...** **The question word** must be **repeated** in the reported question. *(Fragewort muss wiederholt werden.)*

He said, "**Why** didn't you turn off the light?"
He asked **why** I hadn't turned off the light.

She said, "**Where** do you buy your bread?"
She wanted to know **where** I bought my bread.

He said, "**How long** did you stay in America?"
He was interested in **how long** I had stayed in America.

She said, "**Whose** car is this opposite the phone box?"
She inquired **whose** car that was opposite the phone box.

2. Without a question word we must use *if* or *whether* (ob)

He said, "Are you afraid?"
He wanted to know ***if / whether*** I was afraid.

She said, "Didn't you see him at Jim's party?"
She asked ***if / whether*** I hadn't seen him at Jim's party.

3. Questions with *shall*: more solutions are possible, depending on what you want to express.
(Mehrere Lösungen sind möglich, je nachdem, was man ausdrücken will.)

Lucy said, "Where **shall** we be this time tomorrow?"
Lucy wondered where we / they **would** be that time the following day.
*(... wo sie wohl sein **würde** ...)*

Tom said, "Where **shall** I park my car?"
Tom wanted to know where he **should** park his car.
*(... wo er sein Auto parken **sollte**.)*

He said, "**Shall** I tell Mark about it?"
He asked if he **was to** tell Mark about it. *(... ob er erzählen **sollte** ...)*
(Anmerkung: **to be to = sollen** wird gerne verwendet, wenn **jemand anderer** möchte, dass etwas getan wird.)
He asked if he **should** tell Mark about it. *(... ob er erzählen **sollte** ...)*

She said, "**Shall** we send him a letter?"
She wanted to know if we / they **were to** send him a letter?
*(... ob sie senden **sollten** ...)*
She wanted to know if we / they **should** send him a letter?
*(... ob sie senden **sollten** ...)*

He said to me, "**Shall** I take you home?"
He **offered** to take me home. *(Er **bot mir an** ...)*
He **suggested** taking me home. (see gerund ☺ IV p 63 f) *(Er **schlug vor** ...)*
He asked me if he **should** take me home. *(... ob er mich heimbringen **sollte**.)*

4. Questions with *will*:

He said, "**Will** the train be on time?"
He asked if the train **would** be on time.

She said, "**Will** you help me with the homework, please?"
She **asked me to** help her with the homework. *(kind request = höfliche Bitte)*

Sam said, "**Will** you have a cup of tea?"
Sam asked if I **would like** (to have) a cup of tea. *(... ob ich **gerne hätte** ...)*
Sam **offered** me a cup of tea. *(anbieten)*
Sam **invited** me for a cup of tea. *(einladen)*

REPORTED QUESTIONS

1. She asked me, "Did you recognize him by his voice?"
2. He said, "Could you get hold of a new TV set for me?"
3. Bob wanted to know, "Why didn't you show the stranger the way?"
4. I wondered, "Did you include a message for Frank?"
5. He asked, "Where shall I find my group again?"
6. He said, "Where did you spend your last holidays?"
7. Billy said to me, "How long has Sally been going steady with Robert?"
8. Linda wanted to know, "Was he frustrated when you told him the truth?"
9. Mum asked, "Will you look after the children, please?"
10. He said, "When are we going to meet at the youth club?"
11. Robert said, "How does she always get away with it?"
12. She asked me, "Shall I come round tomorrow?"
13. I wondered, "Why are you so fed up with school?"
14. He asked, "Did the noise keep you awake?"
15. Sally wanted to know, "How often did she mention his name?"
16. He said, "Will you meet her at the youth club?"
17. She asked me, "Shall we invite her to the party?"
18. Susan wondered, "How often did you date Richard?"
19. Peter wanted to know, "Why are they always making fun of him?"
20. Mary said, "Didn't he really take any notice of Belinda?"
21. Frank wanted to know, "Shall we send him a Christmas card?"
22. The teacher asked, "Why can't you concentrate on your work?"
23. She said to me, "Did you know that Julian has a crush on Linda?"
24. He said, "For how long will they be able to stay in Paris?"
25. Michael wanted to know, "Where do you usually buy your meat?"
26. She wondered, "Where shall I be this time next year?"
27. She asked me, "Whose cap is it?"
28. Mrs Miller wants to know, "Are you thirsty? Would you like some juice?"
29. Mum asked us, "Who has cleared away the mess?"
30. He said, "When shall we be back again?"
31. Mother wanted to know, "How long will the trip last?"
32. Fred said, "Are you sure that they want to introduce school uniforms?"
33. The teacher asked, "How much time did it take you to do your work?"
34. He said, "Is it true that Bill is not at home?"
35. Ben said, "Will you have a drink with me?"
36. She asked me, "From where did they have to flee?"
37. Mrs Peasley wanted to know, "Would you like a sandwich now?"
38. He said, "Did he really refuse to help Mandy with her homework?"
39. She asks me, "Where shall I find a suitable flat?"
40. Phil asked, "Have you already read the novel *The Demon Headmaster*?"

41. He said, "Was your school mag a great success?"
42. We wondered, "Why did she walk off without saying anything?"
43. Nicole wanted to know, "Do you think Pam will hug him?"
44. He said, "Can your teacher take a joke?"
45. She asked me, "Did you see him smile?"
46. The teacher wanted to know, "Who was late for school?"
47. Betty asked, "Did they really kiss under the tree?"
48. He asked me, "May I give you some advice?"
49. He said, "How long will it take you to clean your room?"
50. She asked me, "Which dress should I buy?"
51. Conny wondered, "Does he admire Tom Hanks?"
52. Mandy asked, "How much did you pay for this fantastic pullover?"
53. She wanted to know, "How much did you have to pay for it?"
54. We wondered, "Why shall Simon be grounded?"
55. He said, "Do you think she will love that kind of entertainment?"
56. She asked me, "Whose house is that, just opposite the church?"
57. Mr Brown wanted to know, "Who is whisting? You, Tom?"
58. She asked me, "Was it a delightful evening?"
59. We asked her, "Did you find suitable clothes?"
60. Mrs Pancake wanted to know, "Has she got twins?"
61. Nancy said, "Isn't Phil a real looker?"
62. Grandpa wondered, "Did you manage to fill in the crossword puzzle?"
63. He said, "Whose girlfriend did you see in front of the cinema?"
64. Nick asked, "Have you ever met Lucy's sister?"
65. The teacher wants to know, "Which tribe lives on a reservation?"
66. He said, "Where did the Pilgrim Fathers come from?"
67. I wondered, "How long shall we be away?"
68. Granny wanted to know, "Will the bus be on time?"
69. She asked me, "Will you have a glass of water?"
70. Father said, "What did she want to ask you?"
71. We wondered, "Did he really let her down?"
72. He said, "Whose car broke down on the motorway yesterday?"
73. Peter asked, "Shall I help you tomorrow?"
74. Larry wanted to know, "Where else shall I look for my key?"
75. He said, "What kind of girl is she?"
76. She asked me, "When will you be back again?"
77. Chris wanted to know, "When shall we meet in front of the cinema?"
78. The policeman asked, "Whose car is that blue one over there?"
79. The children asked, "How long are you able to stay under water?"
80. He said, "What happened to Bill?"
81. She asks me, "Why did he refuse to stay any longer?"
82. Sue wanted to know, "How long will your chat last, Mum?"
83. I asked, "Will you introduce me to Mr Smith, please?"

REPORTED COMMANDS

1. Polite command, request: (höflicher Befehl, Bitte)

He said, "Come to me, **please**."
He **asked** me to come to him.
He **begged** me to come to him. *(bitten)*
He **invited** me to come to him. *(einladen)*
He **implored** me to come to him. *(anflehen)*
He **said** politely that I **should** come to him.
He **said** that I **should be so kind as to** come to him. *(... ich sollte doch so nett sein ...)*

2. Normal command:

He said, "Come to me."
He **told** me to come to him.
He **reminded** me to come to him. *(erinnern)*
He **said to** me that I **should** come to him. *(sollen)*
He **said to** me that I **ought to** come to him. *(eigentlich sollen)*
He **said to** me that I **was to** come to him. *(sollen)*

She said, "Keep away from this boy."
She **told** me to keep away from that boy.
She **said to** me that I **should** keep away from that boy.
She **said to** me that I **ought to** keep away from that boy.
She **advised** me to keep away from that boy. *(raten, empfehlen)*
She **recommended** that I keep away from that boy. *(empfehlen)*

He said, "Meet me in Park Road."
He **told** me to meet him in Park Road.
He **wanted** me to meet him in Park Road.
He **said** (to me) that we **should** meet in Park Road.
He **said** that I **was to** meet him in Park Road.

He said, "Let's meet in half an hour."
He **suggested** meet**ing** in half an hour.
He **suggested** that we **should** meet in half an hour.

3. Strong command:

He shouted at us, "Come at once!"
He **shouted at** us to come at once.
He **screamed at** us to come at once.
He **urged** us to come at once. *(drängen, darauf dringen)*
He **commanded** us to come at once. *(befehlen)*
He **ordered** us to come at once. *(befehlen)*

4. Negative command:

He said, "Don't move boys!"
He **told / commanded / ordered** the boys **not to** move.
He **told** the boys that they **were not to** move.
He **advised** the boys **not to** move.
He **warned** the boys **not to** move.

He said, "Let's go to the snack bar." Susan, "No, let's not."
He **suggested** go**ing** to the snack bar, but Susan **was against it**.
He **suggested** go**ing** to the snack bar, but Susan **refused**.
He **suggested** that we **should** go to the snack bar, but Susan **didn't want to**.

She said, "Let's not tell him about it."
She **suggested** not tell**ing** him about it.
She **suggested** that we **should** not tell him about it.

REPORTED COMMAND

1. He screamed, "Stop that nonsense at once!"
2. He advised us, "Don't talk to this man."
3. She said, "Have a look at your mistakes again and correct them."
4. She said to me, "Please take this letter to the post office for me."
5. He suggested, "Let's go for a walk in the park."
6. The man said, "Keep away from this dangerous dog."
7. Lucy said, "Don't call him a liar."
8. He said, "Let's keep it a secret." – We answered, "No, let's not."
9. Mum said, "Take your raincoat with you, Ben!"
10. Sheila said, "Let's take the nine o'clock bus."
11. The teacher said to us, "Sit down now!"
12. She said to us, "Please open the window!"
13. Mother said to me, "Please help me with the cooking."
14. Frank warned us, "Don't be late tomorrow!"
15. Mum came in and said, "Shut the windows because it is so cold."
16. Luke said to his dad, "Please give me some money."
17. Bill said to his brother, "Leave me alone! I don't want to be disturbed."
18. I said to Mary, "Go to Mrs Fisher and bring her some apples."
19. Father said to Tom, "You mustn't watch TV now."
20. The policeman said, "Show me your driving licence."
21. Mum said to me, "Please get some cake for our guests."
22. The teacher said to him, "Don't argue with your parents!"
23. Sally said to me, "Write to me as soon as you are in Paris."
24. "Hands up," the burglar shouted.
25. "Hurry up now!" Mandy shouted.
26. The teacher said to us, "Don't speak until you are asked to."
27. Mum said to dad, "Don't drive so fast."
28. Mum shouted, "Stop that noise at once!"
29. She said to me, "Don't forget to answer Linda's letter."
30. Mum always says to Tom, "Be careful and don't run across the street."
31. Dad said to Bill, "Please get me some scissors."
32. Mr Smith said to me, "Don't forget to call Mrs Roberts."
33. Mum said to Rita, "Watch the cake and don't let it burn."
34. My sister said to mum, "Please prepare dinner now."
35. Our teacher said to us, "Write a book report on *Mathilda* by R. Dahl."
36. Mum said to Phil, "Take off your coat. It's too warm in here."
37. The policeman shouted at the man, "Get out of your car! Quick!"
38. "Open your suitcase," said the customs officer.
39. The detective said to the driver, "Follow that taxi quickly."
40. Mrs Swan said to her son, "Don't jump like mad."
41. He begged me, "Wait for me in front of the cinema."

42. Sue told her mum, "Don't forget to feed the mice and give them water."
43. Mum said to Nick, "Don't eat too many sweets. It's bad for your teeth."
44. Father said to mum, "Buy two tickets for the concert, please."
45. Dad said to Ben, "Take the dog for a walk now."
46. His secretary said to me, "Wait here until we call you."
47. Mr Smith said to his son, "Cut the grass, please."
48. Mum said to Paul, "Go to the hairdresser's."
49. Lucy said to Mark, "Please take me home now."
50. Granny said to Laura, "Open the letter and read what Mrs Smith has written."
51. The woman said to the boy, "Wait here until your mum comes back."
52. Mum shouted at Joe, "Look what you've done!"
53. Dad said to Bill, "Lock the door twice, please."
54. Mum said to Larry, "Don't use your fingers! Eat with your fork and knife!"
55. Mum said to Tom, "Do your homework quickly and carefully."
56. Mrs Manson said to mum, "Please keep the book as long as you wish."
57. Mum said to Sue, "Wipe the ketchup off your mouth and fingers."
58. Granny said to Joe, "Wash your hands before dinner."
59. Mum said to dad, "Don't forget to buy some bread for the weekend."
60. The policeman said to me, "Take the first turning on the left."
61. The doctor said to me, "You must remain in bed. You've got the flu."
62. Mum said to her son, "Try to behave well."
63. The doctor said, "Please take a seat, Mrs Brown."
64. Grandfather said to Jim, "Don't interrupt me when I'm speaking."
65. Nick said to Robert, "Tell her the truth."
66. Clare said to Eric, "Don't leave me alone!"
67. Mum said to Pam, "Comb your hair and change your shirt."
68. Dad said to Bob, "Wipe the mustard off your shirt."
69. Father said to his family, "Fasten your seat belts!"
70. Mum always says to us, "Look both ways before you cross the street."
71. Mrs Nigel said to us, "Don't smoke in here, please!"
72. Mum said to Mrs Stone, "Have another slice of cake."
73. Mum shouted at Bill, "Don't lean out of the window."
74. Mum said to granny, "Be careful! Mind the steps!"
75. The sign said, "Don't pick flowers in the park."
76. Mum said to dad, "Please buy a nice birthday present for your aunt."
77. The woman said to the children, "Watch out! A car is coming!"
78. Mum said, "Children, go to bed now."
79. Mrs Fisher said to me, "Let's have a cup of tea together."
80. Mum said to Brian, "Don't dye your hair blue or father will be angry."
81. Stella said to me, "Please call me at six."
82. Dad said to his friend, "Have a look at today's newspaper. There's an interesting article in it."
83. Mary and Ken said, "Let's join the drama club!"

REPORTED SPEECH: EXCLAMATIONS

Various constructions are possible. *(Verschiedene Konstruktionen sind möglich.)*
Study the following examples:

Help!	She **called for help**.
Thank you!	Bill **thanked me**.
Good morning!	They **wished** us **a good morning**.
Congratulations!	He **congratulated me**.
Fool!	She **called him a fool**.
No!	He **refused**.
Yes!	She **agreed**.
Yes, I'll come!	He **agreed to come**.
Hello!	They **greeted me**.
How awful!	He said that **it was awful**.

What a terrible snowstorm!
He **expressed his dismay at** the terrible snowstorm.
He **complained about** that terrible snowstorm.

What a lovely pond you've got!
He **observed what** a lovely pond we had. *(bemerken, feststellen)*
He **expressed his admiration for** our pond. *(seine Bewunderung ausdrücken)*
He **commented on** what a lovely pond we had. *(sich äußern)*

Goodness me! I've torn my trousers!
She **complained of** hav<u>ing</u> torn her trousers. (also see ☺ IV, GERUND p 66)
She **was shocked at** hav<u>ing</u> torn her trousers. (also see ☺ IV, GERUND p 67)
She **was annoyed at** hav<u>ing</u> torn her trousers. (also see ☺ IV, GERUND p 67)
(Sie war verärgert, weil sie ihre Hose zerrissen hatte.)

What a nice present!
She **exclaimed** what a nice present it was.

What a wonderful day!
He said (that) **it was** a wonderful day.
He **exclaimed** what a wonderful day it was.

What a fantastic book!
He said (that) **it was** a fantastic book.
He **commented on how** fantastic the book was. *(bemerken, äußern)*

REPORTED SPEECH: SPECIAL CASES

After
wish
I would rather / 'd rather *(es wäre mir lieber)*
as if
if only
it is time *(es ist Zeit)*
it is about time *(es ist Zeit)*
it is high time *(es ist höchste Zeit)*
suppose *(angenommen)*
supposing *(angenommen)*

you can use either **past tense** for **present situations**
or **past perfect tense** for **past situations**.

In **reported speech** **past tense** after **wish, would rather, as if, if only** etc.
remains unchanged. *(die past tense nach wish ... bleibt unverändert)*
(Anmerkung: Diese past tense ist der grammatikalischen Funktion nach eigentlich ein subjunctive, ein Konjunktiv, aber es reicht vollkommen, wenn du dir past tense merkst.)

In <u>written and formal</u> *(geschriebenem und formellem)* English you prefer **were**
for all persons, in <u>spoken, informal</u> *(gesprochenem, informellem, alltäglichem)*
English **was**.

Examples:

She was sure, "Ben *wishes* he **were / was** me." (present situation)
She was sure that Ben *wish<u>ed</u>* he **were / was** her.

Sally told us, "I *wish* I **were / was** thinner." (present situation)
Sally told us that she *wish<u>ed</u>* she **were / was** thinner.

Bob said, "I *wish* I **were / was** you." *(Ich wünschte, ich wäre du.)*
(present situation)
Bob said that he *wish<u>ed</u>* he **were / was** me.

She said, "*I'd rather* Tom **went** with us." (present situation)
She said that *she'd rather* Tom **went** with them.

Sue said, "*I'd rather* he **came** at six."
Sue confessed that *she'd rather* he **came** at six.

He said, "Tim acts *as if* he **were / was** totally crazy." (present situation)
He complained that Tim act<u>ed</u> *as if* he **were / was** totally crazy.

She said, "*If only* I **could** forget him!" (present situation)
She remarked *that she wished* she **could** forget him.

He said to us, "*It is high time* we **left** now." (present situation)
He said to us that *it <u>was</u> high time* we / they **left** then.
He said to us that *it <u>was</u> high time* for us to leave then.

She reminded us, "*It is about time* we **began** to cook." (present situation)
She reminded us that *it <u>was</u> about time* we **began** to cook.

She said, "*Suppose* you **met** him at Nancy's party!" (present situation)
She told me *to imagine what it would be like if* I **met** him at Nancy's party.

She said, "I *wish* I **had known** that before." (past situation)
She said that she *wish<u>ed</u>* she **had known** that before.

He said, "I *wish* I **had had** a better job." *(hätte gehabt)* (past situation)
He said that he *wish<u>ed</u>* he **had had** a better job.

Simon said, "I *wish* I **had been** stronger." (past situation)
Simon said that he *wish<u>ed</u>* he **had been** stronger.

She said, "*If only* the weather **had been** fine we **could have stayed** longer." (past situation)
She complained that *if only* the weather **had been** fine they **could have stayed** longer.

He said , "*I'd rather* you **had been** on time." (past situation)
(du wärest pünktlich gewesen)
He said *he'd rather* you / I / we **had been** on time.
He said *he would have preferred* for you to **have been** on time.

She said, "*I'd rather* you **had paid** the bill on Friday." (past situation)
She said *she'd rather* I **had paid** the bill on Friday.

He said, "Bill acted *as if* he **had lost** his mind." (past situation)
(als hätte er den Verstand verloren)
He complained that Bill <u>had acted</u> *as if* he **had lost** his mind.

SAY OR TELL

Say + *to* + person
Say *(that)*

He **said** *to* **me** that I was late.
What did she **say** *to* you?
She **said** *that* we were in time.
She **said** we were wrong.

Keep in mind:

> **say** a poem *(aufsagen)*
> **say** for myself *(zu meiner Verteidigung)*
> **say** the word *(ja sagen)*
> It goes without **saying** that ... *(es versteht sich von selbst)*
> Have you **said** your **say** yet? *(Bist du damit fertig, was du zu sagen hast?)*
> Let her have her **say**! *(Lass sie einmal was sagen!)*
> that is to **say** *(sozusagen)*
> What do you **say** to a cup of tea? *(Wie wäre es mit ...)*
> let's **say** *(sagen wir einmal)*
> I have some **say** in the matter. *(Ich habe dazu wohl auch noch was zu sagen.)*
> You have no **say** in this matter. *(kein Mitspracherecht)*
> She always has the final **say**. *(das letzte Wort)*
> Are you **saying** that ... *(meinst du damit, dass ...)*
> Who shall I **say**? *(Wen darf ich melden?)*
> That's not for me to **say**. *(Das kann ich nicht entscheiden.)*
> Is he clever? – I should **say** so! *(Na und ob!)*
> If you don't like that, **say** so! *(sag's nur!)*
> So **saying**, she left. *(Mit diesen Worten ging sie.)*
> **say** after somebody *(nachsprechen)*
> It **says** in the newspaper ... *(In der Zeitung steht ...)*
> What does your horoscope **say**?
> The weather forecast **says** that ... *(Der Wetterbericht meldet ...)*
> What does your watch **say**? *(Wie spät ist es?)*
> You don't **say**! *(Was du nicht sagst!)*
> Never let it be **said** that he didn't try his best.
> *(Es soll keiner sagen können, dass er nicht sein Bestes versucht hätte.)*

tell + person

He **told** *me* that he had a car.
She **told** *Bill* that he had a good mark.
What did Simon **tell** *you*?

Keep in mind:

> **Tell** the future
> **tell** the news
> **tell** the world *(jedem erzählen)*
> **tell** the truth *(Wahrheit)*
> **tell** the difference *(Unterschied feststellen)*
> **tell** the time *(die Uhr kennen)*
> **tell** somebody the way
> **tell** a story
> **tell** a secret
> **tell** lies *(Lügen)*
> **tell** tales *(Gerüchte)*
> **tell** right from wrong *(Recht und Unrecht unterscheiden)*
> **tell** somebody off *(schimpfen)*
> to be **told** off for special duty *(abkommandiert werden für / zu einem Spezialeinsatz)*
> **tell** on somebody *(jemandes Gesundheit beeinträchtigen; jem. verpetzen)*
> I **told** you so! *(Ich warnte dich!)*
> **Tell** me another! *(Wer's glaubt, wird selig!)*
> You can never **tell**. *(Man kann nie wissen.)*
> Can you **tell** her from her twin sister? *(unterscheiden)*
> There's no use **telling** her anything. *(Es nützt nichts, ihr irgendetwas zu sagen.)*
> How did he **tell** which button to press? *(Wie stellte er fest ...)*
> How can I **tell** ? *(Wie / woher soll ich das wissen?)*
> There's no **telling** what may happen! *(Man kann nie wissen ...)*
> I'll **tell** you what ... *(Ich werde dir mal was sagen ..., Weißt du was ...?)*
> No words can **tell** how sad she is. *(Es lässt sich nicht mit Worten sagen ...)*
> more than words can **tell** *(mehr als man mit Worten sagen kann)*
> You can **tell** that she's getting worried. *(Man sieht es ihr an, dass sie ...)*
> You are **telling** me! *(Wem sagen Sie das!)*
> a **telling** speech *(beeindruckende Rede)*
> a **telling** colour *(schreiende Farbe)*
> a **telling** argument *(effektvoll, überzeugend)*

FILL IN THE CORRECT FORMS OF SAY OR TELL

1. He .... , "The boys are coming."
2. She .... me, "Oliver hasn't come yet."
3. She .... , "My umbrella is leaking."
4. She .... me that he hadn't come yet.
5. He .... that the door was open when he arrived.
6. Father .... to her that she was wrong.
7. He .... me that I was wrong.
8. She .... us to sit down and to be quiet.
9. The man .... us how to open the window.
10. She always .... us lies.
11. Please .... me the truth.
12. He always .... the truth.
13. He .... us about his adventures in India.
14. He .... us how dangerous his trip was.
15. She .... her story to everybody she met.
16. Be polite and .... "Please"!
17. Did you .... anything to me?
18. He .... that his friend's name was Miller.
19. Everyone .... how fine she looked after her holiday.
20. He .... me to keep quiet about this accident.
21. He .... me that I should keep quiet about it.
22. I've something to .... to you.
23. I've something to .... you.
24. I wouldn't .... "no" to a glass of beer now.
25. The girl was .... a poem.
26. He .... me why he had gone away.
27. Mary .... me how to prepare for the test.
28. It goes without .... that country life is healthier than town life.
29. I haven't got anything to .... for myself.
30. What can you .... to defend yourself, Peter?
31. There is no .... him anything.
32. Who can .... the difference between them?
33. I only came round to .... "goodbye" to you.
34. I came to .... what I think of you.
35. You've only got to .... the word and the car is yours.
36. She hasn't a good word to .... for anybody.
37. Have you .... your .... yet?
38. Pay it by May 10th, that is to .... by three weeks tomorrow.
39. What do you .... to a walk?
40. You may learn to play the violin in, let's .... , three years.

41. You needn't listen to him, he hasn't got very much to ....
42. Pam .... the news to everybody.
43. I gave him my address and .... him my name.
44. She .... that she loved me.
45. She wouldn't .... why she did so.
46. .... me where you live.
47. Surely I have some .... in the matter.
48. I can't .... you how happy I am!
49. It is impossible to .... him anything because he thinks he knows everything best.
50. I .... you that you'd miss the bus, didn't I?
51. Please .... me a story.
52. She .... the police about the accident.
53. Did you .... that I was wrong? I must .... you that you were right.
54. Are you .... that he is the man we are looking for?
55. If he asks, ... him!
56. I'll .... you what you can do for her.
57. Don't complain now, I .... you so!
58. Please don't .... , "I .... you so".
59. .... me another!
60. ".................. the truth", he .... to me.
61. She always .... tales about everybody!
62. Do what I .... you.
63. .... him to wait outside.
64. He .... a lot of nonsense.
65. You must do what you are ....
66. Can you .... Luke from his twin brother?
67. How can you .... which is which ?
68. Can little Sue .... the time yet?
69. Can you .... me what time it is, please?
70. You can never .... if he is in time or not!
71. Ten men were .... off for special duty.
72. There's no .... what may happen!
73. That young man needs to be .... off.
74. Sarah, you promised not to .... anybody!
75. How can you .... that he .... lies!
76. What have you got to .... for yourself?
77. Does she like Frank? – I should .... so!
78. We should have .... him earlier.
79. He fears that the doctor .... him the truth.
80. She is .... to be a very good teacher.

81. Will he arrive tomorrow? – Yes, he .... so yesterday.
82. Please .... the word and let me go!
83. .... her not to wait for me.
84. He .... to us that he would be at the headquarters at nine.
85. I'm not against your suggestion, but that's not for me to ....
86. Must you always .... on me?
87. He .... Bill to wait in front of the cinema.
88. If you don't want to accept his invitation, ... so!
89. She .... us how to get to the shelter.
90. If you .... her a secret, she .... the world.
91. Sally was really impressed by the concert, but Larry .... nothing.
92. Please do what you are .... !
93. He loves her more than words can ....
94. .... after me, "I will love you till I die!"
95. He .... me to keep quiet about his treatment in hospital.
96. Please don't .... Peter anything about what happened.
97. There is no .... him anything. He always knows best.
98. I'll .... you what, let's write a school mag!
99. Betty can't .... trashy books from good ones.
100. His lifestyle is .... on him.
101. He .... that Ben's father suffered a heart attack.
102. She .... Bill that she wanted to get to know him.
103. He .... that his parents had come home unexpectedly.
104. We didn't .... the headmaster about the broken window.
105. She .... us that she would play a small part in some soap opera.
106. He .... that the castle was haunted and that a maniac lived there.
107. He .... us off for being late.
108. I was .... to stay in bed for a week.
109. Harry .... that the new restaurant was cheap.
110. Did he .... you his name?
111. She .... to Linda that she didn't like Sam.
112. It goes without .... that milk cartons must be collected.
113. We'll meet at the camping site at four, that is to .... in six hours.
114. Are you .... that Frank doesn't date Nancy any more?
115. You can .... that she is pretty nervous.
116. You don't ....! Richard has got a stepsister!
117. The weather forecast .... that it'll be fine tomorrow.
118. .... me the truth! Does he meet another girl?
119. Little Monica can .... the time.

HOW TO TRANSLATE „LASSEN"

> **1.** *lassen, aufhören*: **stop, keep from, keep on, cannot help, drop, not to do, leave, leave off**

Stop crying.
He can't **stop** smoking. *(Er kann mit dem Rauchen nicht aufhören.)*
He can't **keep from** drinking. *(Er kann mit dem Trinken nicht aufhören.)*
He **keeps on** doing it. *(Er kann es nicht lassen.)*
He **can't help** it. *(Er kann es nicht lassen.)*
Let's **drop** the whole idea. *(Lassen wir das Ganze sein.)*
If you don't want to, then **don't**. *(Wenn du nicht willst, dann lass es.)*
Let's **leave** it. *(Lassen wir das.)*
Leave off teasing the dog! *(Hör auf, den Hund zu necken.)*

> **2.** *zurücklassen, alleine lassen, überlassen, auslassen, verlassen, anlassen*: **leave**

I **left** my umbrella on the bus.
You may **leave** your suitcase here.
She **left** all her luggage **behind**. *(Sie ließ all ihr Gepäck zurück.)*
When I'm on holiday I **leave** my key **with** the neighbours.
He **left** a message on the kitchen table.
He always **leaves** his things **about**. *(Er lässt immer seine Dinge herumliegen.)*
Please **leave** the window open.
I **left** the light on. *(Ich ließ das Licht brennen.)*
Leave me **alone**, please. *(Lass mich allein / in Ruhe, bitte.)*
Leave Frank **to** himself. *(Lass Frank allein / in Ruhe.)*
Leave that / it (**up**) **to** me. *(Lass das mir über. / Überlassen Sie das mir.)*
Let's **leave** it **at** that. *(Lassen wir es dabei.)*
Leave this **aside**. *(Lass das beiseite.)*
You must **leave** one page **blank**. *(Du musst eine Seite freilassen.)*
She **left out** one exercise.
He **left** us at eight.
Leave your shoes on. *(Lassen Sie Ihre / Lass deine Schuhe an.)*
He **left** it unsaid. *(Er ließ es ungesagt.)*

3. *(zu)lassen, erlauben*:	let, allow, permit

Let me go to Linda's party.
Please **allow** us to go to the cinema.
He **permitted** them to stay a bit longer.

4. *im Stich lassen*:	let somebody down / leave in the lurch
aus den Augen lassen:	let out of sight / keep an eye on
nachlassen:	let up
fallen lassen:	drop
sich gehen lassen:	let oneself go
herauslassen:	let out

Don't **let** me **down** now. *(Lass mich jetzt nicht im Stich.)*
He **left** her **in the lurch**. *(Er ließ sie im Stich.)*
Don't **let** the children **out of** your **sight**. *(Lass die Kinder nicht aus den Augen.)*
The rain was **letting up**, so we could go for a walk. *(Der Regen ließ nach ...)*
He is **letting up** at school. His marks are getting worse.
(Er lässt in der Schule nach.)
She **dropped** the glass. *(Sie ließ das Glas fallen.)*
Whenever she drinks too much, she **lets** herself **go**.
She **let out** a scream of pain. *(Sie ließ einen Schmerzensschrei los.)*
I must **let out** my clothes. *(herauslassen, weiter machen)*

5. *veranlassen,*	make + object + infinitive without *to*,
dazu bringen:	to see to it, order, to arrange for,
	to lead / cause somebody to do something

His jokes always **make** me laugh. *(... bringen mich immer zum Lachen.)*
What **made** him do that? *(Was veranlasste ihn, das zu tun?)*
The snowstorm **made** them return.
(Der Schneesturm veranlasste sie zurückzugehen.)
She **saw to it** that the house was cleaned. *(Sie ließ das Haus putzen. =*
Sie veranlasste, dass das Haus geputzt wurde.)
He **ordered** the fence to be mended. *(Er ließ den Zaun flicken. =*
Er veranlasste, dass der Zaun geflickt wird / wurde.)
He **arranged for** measures to be taken. *(Er ließ Maßnahmen ergreifen.)*
(Also see: ***passive infinitive*** ☺ IV p 53 ff)
The circumstances **lead / cause** him to sign the paper.
(Die Umstände veranlassen ihn das Schriftstück zu unterschreiben.)

> **6. *veranlassen*:** have + object + past participle
> (The **doer** is **not mentioned**.)
> *(Die **Person**, die den **Auftrag ausführt**, wird **nicht erwähnt**.)*

I **have** my car **washed**. *(Ich lasse mein Auto waschen.)*
She **has** her house **cleaned**. *(Sie lässt ihr Haus putzen.)*
We **have** our garden fence **repaired**.
(Wir lassen unseren Gartenzaun reparieren.)
He **had** his hair **cut**. *(Er ließ sich die Haare schneiden.)*
You **should have** your room **painted**.
(Du solltest dein Zimmer ausmalen lassen.)
She **will have** her new dress **let out**.
(Sie wird ihr neues Kleid weitermachen lassen.)
She **will have** to have her new dress **let out**.
(Sie wird ihr neues Kleid weitermachen lassen müssen.)

Attention:

Mind the word order:
  have + object + past participle = lassen
  have + past participle + object = present perfect!

  had + object + past participle = ließ
  had + past participle + object = past perfect!

Compare:

I **have** my hair **cut**. *(Ich lasse meine Haare schneiden.)*
I **have cut** my hair. *(Ich habe mir meine Haare [selbst] geschnitten.)*

You **should have** your socks **mended**.
(Du solltest deine Socken stopfen lassen.)
You **should have mended** your socks.
(Du hättest deine Socken [selbst] stopfen sollen.)

He **had** his house **sold**. *(Er ließ sein Haus verkaufen.)*
He **had sold** his house. *(Er hatte sein Haus verkauft.)*

7. Keep in mind:

That's enough of that kind of remark! (Lass solche Bemerkungen!)

If you must, you must! (Tu, was du nicht lassen kannst!)

He left the casino with his pockets a lot lighter. (Er hat viel Geld im Casino gelassen.)

We have got to give him that! (Das muss man ihm lassen / zugestehen!)

She runs water into the bath. (Sie lässt Wasser in die Wanne ein.)

She had a checkup. (Sie ließ sich untersuchen.)

He had a tooth out. (Er ließ sich einen Zahn ziehen.)

I let him know that we would arrive at nine. (Ich ließ ihm ausrichten ...)

She didn't show anything. (Sie hat sich nichts anmerken lassen.)

He grows a beard. (Er lässt sich einen Bart wachsen.)

She grows her hair. (Sie lässt sich das Haar wachsen.)

He kept us waiting. (Er ließ uns warten.)

Frank was not to be persuaded. (Frank ließ sich nicht überreden.)

I won't be lied to! (Ich lasse mich nicht belügen.)

The window opens easily. (Das Fenster lässt sich leicht öffnen.)

The book is hard to translate. (Das Buch lässt sich schwer übersetzen.)

That's possible. / That can be done. (Das lässt sich machen.)

Nothing can be done about it. (Das lässt sich nicht mehr ändern.)

That's all right, I'll pay! (Lass es sein, ich bezahle!)

His handwriting **leaves** much to be desired. (Seine Handschrift lässt sehr zu wünschen übrig.)

TRANSLATE

1. Er ließ sein Fahrrad im Park liegen.
2. Lassen wir das.
3. Mutter lässt ihn nicht zur Party gehen.
4. Bitte, lass die Tür offen.
5. Lass es sein! Ich lade dich ein!
6. Ihr Ehemann ließ vieles ungesagt.
7. Bitte, lass den Schlüssel stecken.
8. Er lässt uns nie allein auf Urlaub fahren.
9. Du kannst deinen Mantel hierlassen.
10. Bitte, lasst mich jetzt allein und lasst mich arbeiten.
11. Ihr müsst zwei Seiten freilassen.
12. Er ließ sie im Stich, als sie ihr Baby bekam.
13. Sie ließ den Hund nicht aus den Augen.
14. Ich lasse das euch über, ob ihr kommt oder nicht.
15. Du hast Nummer sieben ausgelassen.
16. Er wurde veranlasst, die Hausübung noch einmal zu schreiben.
17. Dieser Film sollte euch zum Nachdenken bringen.
18. Die Tür lässt sich nicht leicht öffnen.
19. Der Tod seines Großvaters veranlasste ihn heimzukehren.
20. Sie ließ sich ein neues Kleid nähen.
21. Dein Witz brachte alle zum Lachen.
22. Er sollte seine Haare schneiden lassen.
23. Das schlechte Wetter veranlasste uns, weiter in den Süden zu fahren.
24. Sie veranlasste, dass die Teppiche gesaugt werden.
25. Lass die Probleme für eine Weile beiseite.
26. Was, um Gottes willen, brachte sie dazu, ihren Mann zu verlassen?
27. Was brachte ihn zum Weinen?
28. Das schöne Wetter veranlasste uns, einen Spaziergang zu machen.
29. Er ließ sein Fahrrad putzen.
30. Wir müssen unser Zimmer wieder ausmalen lassen.
31. Tom hat sich einen Bart wachsen lassen.
32. Der Arzt ließ uns nicht lange warten.
33. Du kannst deinen Hut auflassen.
34. Sie lässt in der Schule nach.
35. Sie lassen in ihrem Garten ein Glashaus bauen.
36. Er ließ seine Geldtasche im Geschäft liegen.
37. Das lässt sich nicht mehr ändern.
38. Tu, was du nicht lassen kannst!
39. Er ließ Maßnahmen ergreifen, um den Flüchtlingen zu helfen.
40. Robert ließ das hübsche Mädchen nicht mehr aus den Augen.

41. Sie sollte ihren Mantel putzen lassen.
42. Er ist ein toller Schifahrer! Das muss man ihm lassen!
43. Frau Smith ließ ihre Wohnung verkaufen.
44. Vater ließ sich einen Zahn ziehen.
45. Vater musste sich einen Zahn ziehen lassen.
46. Ich befürchte, wir haben das Licht brennen lassen.
47. Sie war sehr traurig, aber sie hat sich nichts anmerken lassen.
48. Mutter ließ sich nicht überreden, uns zur Party gehen zu lassen.
49. Bitte, lass ihm ausrichten, dass ich mich nicht belügen lasse.
50. Du lässt immer deine Schuhe herumliegen!
51. Er ließ seinen Schirm im Geschäft.
52. Wie werden das Gras mähen lassen müssen.
53. Du solltest zum Nachdenken gebracht werden.
54. Ich brachte ihn zum Weinen.
55. Sie können den Mantel anlassen.
56. Bitte lass uns bei Sarah über Nacht bleiben.
57. Der Schneesturm ließ nach, daher konnten wir hinausgehen.
58. Sie ist ein bezauberndes Mädchen. Das muss man ihr lassen!
59. Nach dem Verkehrsunfall ließ er sein Auto in der Wiese stehen.
60. Bitte, lass den Ofen nicht aus den Augen!
61. Er braucht deine Hilfe! Lass ihn jetzt nicht im Stich.
62. Der Wind lässt nach.
63. Er ließ den Fernseher leiser stellen.
64. Du kannst das Licht brennen lassen, wenn du dich fürchtest.
65. Bitte, lasse Wasser in die Wanne ein.
66. Dieser Satz lässt sich nicht leicht übersetzen.
67. Er liebt das Glücksspiel und lässt viel Geld im Casino.
68. Die Leute haben den Müll auf der Straße liegen lassen.
69. Du hast eine ganze Nummer ausgelassen.
70. Bitte, lassen Sie Ihre Schuhe an!
71. Ich habe meinen Einkaufszettel zu Hause gelassen.
72. Lassen Sie mich das machen!
73. Er verließ uns um ungefähr sieben.
74. Wenn du nicht magst, lass es sein!
75. Lassen wir das Ganze sein!
76. Bitte, lass nicht immer deine Hefte am Küchentisch liegen.
77. Sie ließ die Vase fallen.
78. Kannst du um elf kommen? – Ja, das lässt sich machen.
79. Sie ließ weitere Maßnahmen gegen das Rauchen im Büro ergreifen.
80. Er kann das Rauchen nicht lassen.
81. Er kann es nicht lassen.
82. Lassen wir es dabei: Wir treffen uns bei Jim.

83. Lass nicht all deine Sachen herumliegen!
84. Deine Handschrift lässt sehr zu wünschen übrig!
85. Simon ließ sich nicht überreden, länger zu bleiben.
86. Lasst uns in den Süden fahren.
87. Erlaube mir bis um Mitternacht auszubleiben.
88. Er ließ die Schüler eine Stunde früher nach Hause gehen.
89. Lass das Nörgeln!
90. Er kann das Bergsteigen nicht lassen.
91. Er muss sich den neuesten Computer kaufen. Er kann es nicht lassen.
92. Er kann das Tennisspielen nicht lassen.
93. Er soll es lassen, wenn er nicht will.
94. Sie kann es nicht lassen, immer wieder mit ihm auszugehen.
95. Immer wenn sie ihn braucht, lässt er sie im Stich.
96. Hör auf sie zu pflanzen.
97. Er lässt seine Mutter immer seine Sachen wegräumen.
98. Ich habe meinen Koffer im Zug gelassen.
99. Ich lasse ihn damit nicht davonkommen.
100. Es war peinlich, dass ich sie habe warten lassen.
101. Er ist eine gutaussehende Person. Das muss man ihm lassen!
102. Wenn du mich jetzt in Ruhe lässt, helfe ich dir später beim Kreuzworträtsel.
103. Lassen wir das nun beiseite und konzentrieren wir uns auf die Hausübung.
104. Wenn wir in den Ferien sind, lassen wir unsere Mäuse bei den Nachbarn.
105. Sie hinterließ eine kurze Nachricht und ging weg.
106. Machen Sie sich keine Mühe. Überlassen Sie das mir.
107. Lass deine Handschuhe an, es ist kalt.
108. Seit sie fest mit ihm geht, lässt sie ihn nicht mehr aus den Augen.
109. Wie wäre es mit einer Radtour? Der Regen lässt nach.
110. Sie geht gerne mit Bill aus. Er bringt sie immer zum Lachen.
111. Pass auf! Lass die Tasse nicht fallen!
112. Das Gewitter veranlasste sie zu Hause zu bleiben.
113. Er lässt das alte Sofa wegräumen.
114. Sie ließ sich unterm Baum küssen.
115. Der Lehrer ließ uns einen Buchreport schreiben.
116. Der Lehrer ließ einen Buchreport schreiben.
117. Sie veranlassten ihn, Maßnahmen ergreifen zu lassen.
118. Michael sollte seinen Schirm nicht immer irgendwo liegenlassen.
119. Er ließ sich die Haare orange färben.
120. Wenn er mit Sally ausgeht, lässt sie ihn immer lange warten.
121. Wir ließen das Radio an. Bitte geh und schalte es ab.
122. Barbara ließ sich nicht überreden, ihn zu besuchen.
123. Kannst du die Schuhe wegräumen? – Ja, das lässt sich machen.
124. Die Dose lässt sich leicht öffnen.

INFINITIVE WITH TO

> **1.** after **verbs** like   expect, wish, want, refuse *(ablehnen)*, **prefer***,
> agree *(zustimmen)*, **try***, **decide** *(sich entscheiden)*,
> **happen** *(zufällig tun)*, **remember*** *(sich erinnern)*,
> **hesitate** *(zögern)*, **learn**, **promise** *(versprechen)*,
> **regret*** *(bedauern)*, **attempt** *(versuchen)*,
> **manage** *(es schaffen)*, **seem** *(scheinen)*, **hope**.

Examples:

I **hope** *to see* you again.
She **wishes** *to meet* him again.
I **don't want** *to tell* him the truth.
He **refused** *to come*.
She **agrees** *to help* me.
I'll **try** *to repair* it.
He **decided** *to leave*.
I **happened** *to meet* him. *(Ich traf ihn zufällig.)*
I **remember** *to write* her. *(Ich erinnere mich, dass ich ihr schreiben muss.)*
He **hesitated** *to tell* her the truth. *(Er zögerte, ihr die Wahrheit zu sagen.)*

* also see GERUND p 73 ff

> **2.** after **adjectives**

Examples:

I'm **happy** *to meet* you.
He is not **easy** *to understand*.
I'm **sorry** *to say* this.
This riddle is **difficult** *to solve*.
Our house is **easy** *to find*.
She is **easy** *to get* on with. *(Mit ihr ist gut auszukommen.)*
She was **disappointed** *to see* him with another girl. *(enttäuscht)*
The milk is <u>**too**</u> **hot** (for me) *to drink*.
She is <u>**too**</u> **young** *to understand*.
These trousers are <u>**too**</u> **old-fashioned** (for him) *to wear*.

She was **too** tired *to read*.
She is not **so** silly as *to do* this.
Would you be **so** kind as *to open* the window?
Would you be **kind enough** *to go* shopping for me?
It was **cold enough** *to freeze*.
He is **tall enough** *to touch* the ceiling.
You are **old enough** *to know* what to do.

> **3.** after **nouns** that express **a wish, an order ...**
>
> **ability** (Fähigkeit)   **opportunity*** (Gelegenheit)
> **attempt** (Versuch)   **permission** (Erlaubnis)
> **chance***   **possibility*** (Möglichkeit)
> **courage** (Mut)   **reason** (Grund)
> **decision** (Entscheidung)   **refusal** (Weigerung)
> **determination** (Entschluss)   **resolution** (Entschluss)
> **freedom** (Freiheit)   **right** (Recht)
> **idea*** (Idee)   **time**
> **impudence** (Unverschämtheit)   **will** (Wille)
> **intention** (Absicht)   **wish**
> **mood** (Stimmung)

* also see GERUND p 68

Examples:

She told him her **decision** *to go*.
It is **time** *to leave*.
One **possibility** is *to offer* him more money.
They didn't hear his **command** *to run away*.
I'm not in the **mood** *to laugh* now.

4. after **ordinal numbers** *(Ordnungszahlwörtern)* and
superlatives *(3. Steigerungsstufe)* and
the only (thing / one / ones / person / way)

Examples:

He is always **the first** *to come* and **the last** *to go*.
The **best** thing *to do* is *(to) sleep*.
The only one *to come* was Peter.
The only thing *to do* is *(to) study* harder.
Is this really **the only way** *to do* it?
Robert was **the only person** *to complain*.

5. after **What a ...!**

Examples:

What a silly answer *to give*! *(Was für eine dumme Antwort!)*
What a stupid thing *to say*! *(Was für ein Blödsinn, so etwas zu sagen!)*
What a stupid place *to park* your car, Helen!
What a foolish thing *to tell* him about it! *(Was für ein Blödsinn, ihm davon zu erzählen!)*

6. after **as if**

Examples:

He moved his lips **as if** *to say* something.
He looked at her **as if** *to make* fun of her. *(als wollte er sich über sie lustig machen)*

7. after only   to express something negative

(um etwas Negatives, Enttäuschendes auszudrücken).

Examples:

He ran to the car **only *to find*** it empty.
He followed her **only *to see*** her with another man.

8. after in order to *(um zu)*

Examples:

He came **in order *to help*** her.
She sat down **in order *to have*** a cup of tea.

9. after verbs like explain, discover, find out ... we use how to

Examples:

He **explained *how to use*** this machine.
She **discovered *how to open*** the box.

10. infinitive as a subject

Examples:

To start / begin with, we can't afford a new car. *(Um damit anzufangen ...)*
To see him is **to love** him.
To know her is **to adore** her.
To tell the truth, I don't like her. *(Um die Wahrheit zu sagen ...)*
To sum up, we must start again. *(Um zusammenzufassen ...)*

11. **to** alone in order to **avoid repetition**

(to steht alleine, um Wiederholung zu vermeiden)

Examples:

Did you meet him? – No, but I wanted ***to***.
Would you like some tea? – Yes, I'd love ***to***.
I wanted to help him, but I wasn't able ***to***.
Did you speak to him? – No, but I tried ***to***.
Did you water the flowers? – No, but now I'm going ***to***.

12. **negative** infinitive: **not to**

Examples:

He pretended ***not to* know** me.
He decided ***not to* help** her any more.
She promised ***not to* do** it again.
He tried ***not to* get** angry.

INFINITIVE WITHOUT TO

1. after modal verbs (can, may, must, shall, will, should, would, could, might)

I **can** *help* you.
You **may** *come* in.
He **should** *help* me.

Attention: with **need** and **dare** *(wagen)* there are two possibilities: in question and negation.

You **needn't** *say* goodbye.	= You **don't need** *to say* goodbye.
I **dare not** *tell* him the truth.	= I **don't dare** *to tell* him the truth.
I **daren't** *invite* him.	= I **don't dare** *to invite* him.
I **wouldn't dare** *wake* her now	= I **wouldn't dare** *to wake* her now.
Do you **dare** *tell* him?	= Do you **dare** *to tell* him?

2. after following expressions: **had better** *(lieber sollen)*
had / would sooner *(eher, lieber sollen)*
had / would rather *(lieber möchten)*

I **had rather** *not tell* him. *(Ich würde es ihm lieber nicht sagen.)*
He'd **sooner** *die* than *shoot* at a person. *(Er würde eher sterben ...)*
You **had better** *go* now. *(Du solltest lieber jetzt gehen.)*
Tom **would sooner** *play* than study. *(Tom würde eher spielen als lernen.)*

3. after **why not**

Why not *stay* a bit longer?
(Warum sollten wir nicht ein bisschen länger bleiben? =
Bleiben wir doch noch ein bisschen länger!)
Why not *go* for a walk now? *(Wie wär's mit einen Spaziergang?)*

4. The **second** infinitive after **and, or, but, except** is used **without** *to*

We'd like to stay in Vienna first **and** then *go* to Carinthia.
There was nothing to do **but** *wait*.
There was nothing to do **except** *listen* carefully.
He was not sure whether to accept **or** *refuse*.

INFINITIVE WITH OR WITHOUT TO

1. We happened ……….. meet at the school cafeteria.
2. The pupils needn't ……….. hand in their homework tomorrow.
3. Why not ……….. invite Sarah for lunch tomorrow?
4. You had better ……….. leave your dirty shoes outside.
5. You are always the last ……….. hand in your composition.
6. Hurry up! It's time ……….. go.
7. You have the right ……….. refuse if you don't want ……….. come.
8. You must ……….. accept my decision ……….. leave.
9. I'd rather not ……….. go now.
10. What a foolish idea ……….. mention the accident.
11. They want ……….. fly to Paris first and then ……….. go to Lourdes.
12. They managed ……….. use alternative energy instead of nuclear power.
13. She explained how ……….. cook pizza.
14. ……….. tell the truth, I am not very keen on hot chocolate.
15. Sally is the first ……….. deserve the prize.
16. You don't need ……….. tiptoe. The baby isn't asleep.
17. You weren't able ……….. do anything but ……….. be quiet and ……….. wait for an answer.
18. The only thing ……….. do now is ……….. pray.
19. She was too tired ……….. write the letter.
20. Did you see John? – No, but I really wanted ……….. .
21. It was warm enough ……….. take off your coat.
22. He promised not ……….. leave the door open.
23. I'm glad ……….. see you, Mr Grant.
24. Rick was the last ……….. leave the party, and he promised ……….. come back in the morning in order ……….. help us ……….. clean the house.
25. Why not ……….. plant the tree in front of the house?
26. I didn't know whether ……….. laugh or ……….. cry.
27. He attempted ……….. sell his invention.
28. You don't need ……….. tell me a lie.
29. I didn't dare ……….. inform him about our accident.
30. Did you buy a present for mum? – No, but now I'm going ……….. .
31. Why not ……….. have a cup of tea together?
32. ……….. sum up, we must ……….. attract attention with our campaign.
33. She cried as if ……….. move his heart.
34. He found out how ……….. stop the machine.
35. I wouldn't dare ……….. kiss her.
36. He climbed through the window only ……….. find her on the floor.
37. He would sooner ……….. burn his house than ……….. sell it.

INFINITIVE SHORTENS SENTENCES

Der Infinitiv wird auch zur <u>Satzverkürzung</u> verwendet:

The woman *who gave* us this information is Sally's mother.
The woman **to give** us this information is Sally's mother.

Bill is the wrong person *who you should* complain to.
Bill is the wrong person for you **to complain** to.

He was the first man *that* set his foot on the moon.
He was the first man **to set** his foot on the moon.

She was the last *that* paid the bill.
She was the last **to pay** the bill.

He was the only one *that* survived the accident.
He was the only one **to survive** the accident.

I need somebody *that I can* talk to.
I need somebody **to talk** to.

I need a pen *that I can* write with.
I need a pen **to write** with.

I still have some letters *that I must* write.
I still have some letters **to write**.

She hasn't got anything *that she can* wear for the party.
She hasn't got anything **to wear** for the party.

I need something <u>with</u> *which I can* open the tin.
I need something **to open** the tin <u>with</u>.

She was happy *when* she won the prize.
She was happy **to win** the prize.

I'm sorry *that* I kept you waiting.
I'm sorry **to keep** you waiting.

I don't know *where I should* look for my key.
I don't know **where *to look*** for my key.

I can't tell you *how you can* get to the station.
I can't tell you **how *to get*** to the station.

He explained to me *how I should* work.
He explained to me **how *to work***.

I wasn't sure *how long I should* stay.
I wasn't sure **how long *to stay***.

Have you decided *where you are going* to spend your holidays?
Have you decided **where *to spend*** your holidays?

Billy wondered *what he should* do next.
Billy wondered **what *to do*** next.

Anmerkung: Bei zwei verschiedenen Subjekten kann man das <u>zweite</u> Subjekt mit **for** noch extra erwähnen oder zum **einzigen** Subjekt machen.

<u>He</u> is the only person *that <u>you</u> can* talk to.
<u>He</u> is the only person (<u>for you</u>) ***to talk*** to.

There was <u>no interesting film</u> *that <u>you</u> could* watch on TV.
There was no interesting film (<u>for you</u>) ***to watch*** on TV.

There was no thrilling book *that <u>we could</u>* borrow from the library.
There was no thrilling book (<u>for us</u>) ***to borrow*** from the library.

<u>**It**</u> is certain *that <u>she</u> is going* to take the nine o'clock train.
<u>She</u> is certain ***to take*** the nine o'clock train.

<u>**It**</u> is sure *that <u>he</u> will* come in the evening.
<u>**He**</u> is sure ***to come*** in the evening.

INFINITIVE SHORTENS SENTENCES

Rewrite the sentences **using an infinitive construction**.

1. The girl who came to Peter's party is Linda Jones.
2. He was the first man that swam across the Atlantic.
3. I need someone that can show me how the computer works.
4. He still has some exams that he must pass.
5. You really haven't got anything that you could complain about.
6. I need a brush with which I can clean your coat.
7. It was great when we heard that he had won the first prize.
8. I am very sorry that I must say that we can't trust him.
9. Could you please draw a plan of how I can find your house?
10. She explained to Sue how she should use the typewriter.
11. He was not sure how long he would stay with us.
12. Can you tell us where we can find you?
13. We wondered where we should go next.
14. There is no interesting book in the hotel library that I could read.
15. Frank is the only person that I can tell my secrets.
16. She has decided that she will not leave him.
17. It is not sure if he arrives at three.
18. He explained how I should repair the car.
19. He decided that he would not visit her any more.
20. I'd be happy if I could help you.
21. Robert and I haven't got anything that we could talk about.
22. Have you decided which hat you want to buy?
23. This is an important question that we must answer.
24. I need new coloured pencils that I can draw with.
25. It is certain that they try to attract attention.
26. I still have got some presents that I must wrap up.
27. I'd be very pleased if I could meet him.
28. Mrs Grant was the next person that arrived.
29. There was no interesting film that you could watch on TV.
30. I asked how I could get to the airport the fastest.
31. The most important question is what I should do next.
32. It is certain that we are going to meet her in our holidays.
33. If you stretch your arm out of the window it is very dangerous.
34. He followed Linda and saw her enter Joe's flat, which made him sad.
35. He was too fast so we couldn't catch him.
36. I asked when I should leave.
37. The problem is how we can find a nice present for Jim.
38. The desk is too heavy for her. She can't move it.

OBJECT WITH THE INFINITIVE

> **1. Infinitive with *to* after:**
>
> | | | |
> |---|---|---|
> | want | wish | prefer *vorziehen* |
> | (would) like | love | hate |
> | ask | order | tell |
> | command | allow *erlauben* | permit *erlauben* |
> | think | expect *erwarten* | remember |
> | remind | persuade *überreden* | force *zwingen* |
> | get | invite *einladen* | teach (how) |
> | warn | forbid *verbieten* | show (how) |

I **want** *you* **to help** your brother. (*Attention*: **want** is **never** followed by **that**!)
(Ich möchte, <u>**dass du**</u> deinem Bruder hilfst.)

She **wants** *me* **to clean** my room.
(Sie möchte, <u>**dass ich**</u> mein Zimmer putze.)

He **doesn't like** *us* **to be** late.
(Er mag nicht, <u>**dass wir**</u> zu spät kommen.)

She **doesn't want** *him* **to shave** his head.
(Sie möchte nicht, <u>**dass er**</u> sich den Kopf rasiert.)

We **want** *her* **to read** the opening chapter.
(Wir möchten, <u>**dass sie**</u> das Anfangskapitel liest.)

She **tells** *him* **to buy** a new shovel.
(Sie sagt ihm, <u>**dass er**</u> eine neue Schaufel kaufen soll.)

They **expect** *us* **to look up** all the new words.
(Sie erwarten, <u>**dass wir**</u> alle neuen Wörter nachschlagen.)

She **orders** *us* **to empty** the dustbin.
(Sie befiehlt uns, <u>**dass wir**</u> den Mülleimer ausleeren.)

She **hates for** *him* **to say** goodbye so early.
(Sie hasst es, <u>**dass er**</u> sich so früh verabschiedet.)

I **think** *him* **to be** a nice man.
(Ich glaube, <u>**dass er**</u> ein netter Mann ist.)

I'll **get** *the children* **to help** in the garden.
(Ich werde die Kinder dazu bringen ...)

He **taught** *me* **(how) to juggle**.
(Er lehrte mich zu jonglieren.)

She **showed** *me* **how to bake** a cake.
He **forbids** *her* **to smoke** in the living room.
Please **remind** *me* **to post** the letter.

Negative infinitive: not to + verb

I told *her* **not to** be late.

We asked *them* **not to** interrupt.

He warned *me* **not to** play a trick on him.

2. Infinitive without *to* after:	see	hear	watch
	look at	listen to	observe
	notice	feel	let
	make / have (veranlassen)		

We **saw** *them* **come** home in the morning.

Father **heard** *her* **talk** in a low voice.

(Vater hörte sie mit leiser Stimme sprechen.)

We **watched** *the children* **play** in the playground.

Look *at him* **run** like mad.

(Schau ihn an, wie verrückt er läuft.)

Don't **listen to** *her* **nag** all the time.

(Hör ihr nicht zu, wie sie dauernd nörgelt.)

The police **observed** *him* **sell** drugs.

(Die Polizei beobachtete ihn, wie er Drogen verkaufte.)

Mother **noticed** *us* **come** home late.

(Mutter bemerkte uns spät heimkommen.)

I **felt** *the little cat* **tremble**.

(Ich fühlte, wie die kleine Katze zitterte.)

I **felt** *the earth* **shake**.

(Ich fühlte, wie die Erde bebte.)

What **makes** *the inspector* **think** that she is still alive?

(Was lässt den Inspektor denken, dass sie noch am Leben ist?)

Please **let** *me* **go**.

(Bitte, lass mich gehen / in Ruhe.)

I **have** *him* **share** the sweets with me.

(Ich veranlasse ihn, die Süßigkeiten mit mir zu teilen.)

He **has** *them* **write** a summary.

(Er veranlasst sie, eine Zusammenfassung zu schreiben.)

He **made** *her* **cry**. *(Er brachte sie zum Weinen.)*

Mother **makes** *us* **do** the homework before we play.

(Mutter veranlasst uns, die Hausübung zu machen, bevor wir spielen.)

He wanted to **make** *us* **believe** his story.

(Er wollte uns dazu bringen, dass wir seine Geschichte glauben.)

3. Exceptions:

Help may be used **with or without** *to.*

He **helped me write** an adventure story.
He **helped me** *to* **write** an adventure story.

Verbs that **do not** take *to* (see, hear, watch, observe ...)
in the active, take the infinitive **with *to* in the passive**.

We **were seen** *to* **leave** the house.
She **was heard** *to* **open** the gate.
I **was made** *to* cry.
She **was made** *to* **do** her homework again.

Let is <u>never</u> used with *to.*

Let *me* **go** (active).
I **was let go** (passive).

Suggest is **only used** in a **that**-construction. (or with a *gerund* – see page 64)

We **suggest that** he takes the morning train.
I **suggested that** he did the shopping for the weekend.

4. Infinitive with **when, where, how, who, what, which**

I told them **when** *to meet*.
Can you show me **where** *to find* the Palace Hotel?
Please show us **how** *to use* the new computer.
Tell me **who** *to invite* to our party.
She always tells her **what** *to say*.
Don't always tell me **what** *to do*!
She doesn't know **which** dress *to put* on.
I do not know **who** *to ask* for further information.
The problem is **who** *to send* the letter to.

5. Infinitive with **for**

a) after **verbs** like: **ask, wait, call, send, hope, long** *(sich sehnen)*

I asked **for** a strong man **to help** us.
We are waiting **for** the train **to arrive**.
I'm waiting **for** her **to say** "I'm sorry".
Passengers called **for** the ambulance **to take** him to hospital.
They sent **for** the doctor **to come**.
We hoped **for** Frank **to be** in time.
She is longing **for** him **to visit** her.

b) after **nouns, pronouns, adjectives** and **adverbs**

It is time **for** me **to go**.
It took thirty minutes **for** the bus **to come**.
He opened the door **for** her **to leave**.
Tom thinks it is a funny thing **for** a boy **to put** on make up.
Here's something **for** you **to read**.
There was nowhere **for** him **to go**.
It was not necessary **for** her **to hurt** him.
It's not good **for** you **to smoke**.
It's not easy **for** her **to be** a single mother.
It's absurd **for** a man of his age **to go** to the disco.
It's too hot **for** me **to stay** in the sun.
The mouse ran too fast **for** the cat **to catch** it.
Mark's flat isn't big enough **for** the whole family **to live** in.

(For more examples with **too** and **enough** see ☺ IV p 55)

OBJECT WITH INFINITIVE WITH OR WITHOUT TO

1. Our teacher wants us ...... write book reports on our favourite books.
2. She showed her children how ...... do silk painting.
3. I heard him ...... knock at the door.
4. My neighbour expects me ...... look after her flowers carefully.
5. Frank helped me ...... look for the recipe.
6. Linda does everything Frank tells her ...... do.
7. I think her ...... be a very friendly woman.
8. Mother allows her children ...... stay out until dark.
9. The boys were seen ...... climb over the fence.
10. The police observed them ...... deal with drugs.
11. He ordered us ...... be absolutely quiet during his speech.
12. I'd like him ...... stay three more days.
13. I'd hate you ...... go.
14. Only the thought of my exam makes me ...... feel uncomfortable.
15. My neighbour helped me ...... repair my flat tyre.
16. He wanted me ...... write a good story about people living in India.
17. The baby was heard ...... cry in the afternoon.
18. We watched them ...... dance.
19. Simon, let your little brother ...... go!
20. Mother told him ...... buy wine and beer for the guests.
21. What makes you ...... think that he is a liar?
22. Rick taught me how ...... dive.
23. Julian persuaded Liz ...... spend their holidays together.
24. She didn't know who ...... ask.
25. I would prefer you ...... leave at once.
26. She had her ...... wash the dishes and ...... make the beds.
27. We told them not ...... be so loud.
28. She expects her pupils ...... be punctual.
29. Please remind me ...... post the parcel for dad.
30. I felt the strength ...... leave my body.
31. He made her ...... believe that he had no other girlfriend.
32. We heard them ...... slurp their soup loudly.
33. Please let me ...... copy your homework.
34. She forced him not ...... meet Linda again.
35. He always gets her ...... do more housework than he does.
36. I remember him ...... have been fashionably dressed at Simon's party.
37. Her parents forbid her ...... stay out after midnight.
38. I warned him not ...... take a photo of the inhabitants of the slums.
39. Father wishes her ...... accept her aunt's invitation.

40. I listened to them ...... quarrel over a coloured pen.
41. She had Frank ...... mow the grass.
42. We saw him ...... make a fool of himself.
43. Roger asked her ...... give up her life as a prostitute.
44. We were made ...... finish our homework by Friday.
45. I heard her ...... suck the milkshake with her straw.
46. I hate anybody ...... be cruel to children.
47. The shopkeeper ordered the beggar not ...... sit in front of his shop.
48. He showed her how ...... play the guitar.
49. He was heard ...... put the key into the lock.
50. He told the children not ...... touch anything.
51. She'd love him ...... be more charming.
52. I saw them ...... say good bye in tears.
53. Please help me ...... carry the suitcase to the car.
54. We consider our neighbours ...... be good friends.
55. I asked for a nice girl ...... help us.
56. The teacher ordered the pupils ...... cut out cardboard stars.
57. The inhabitants expect the city authority ...... have the parks cleaned.
58. She told us not ...... touch anything in here.
59. The general commanded his soldiers ...... run as fast as they could.
60. She asked me ...... get free-range eggs from the market for her.
61. I saw him ...... eat a bar of chocolate alone.
62. She forbade them ...... plant a tree in front of her kitchen window.
63. She always warned him not ...... hang about with kids that took drugs.
64. Did you see him ...... leave the house in the morning?
65. He told them ...... check in quickly.
66. He wanted me ...... give him some money.
67. Our teacher always expects us ...... do our best.
68. She really wants me ...... forgive her, but I can't accept her excuse.
69. I remember him ...... have been Kate's best friend.
70. She got me ...... help her the whole afternoon.
71. I'd prefer him not ...... take the plane.
72. She heard Tom ...... go upstairs.
73. I thought him ...... be cleverer than that.
74. She expects us ...... keep all the rules in mind.
75. We only heard her ...... whisper something.
76. I won't permit her ...... use my new car.
77. Mr Brunner orders the kids ...... clean their classroom properly.
78. Tom expects us ...... pick him up at the airport.
79. We invited him .... come to our garden party.

TRANSLATE USING INFINITIVE CONSTRUCTIONS

Attention: In some cases an infinitive construction is not possible!

1. Ich möchte, dass du mir im Garten hilfst.
2. Er schlug mir vor, dass ich weniger Zucker und Fett essen sollte.
3. Sie zieht es vor, heute zu Hause zu bleiben.
4. Vater befahl mir, das Gras zu mähen und mit Rex spazieren zu gehen.
5. Ich hätte gerne, dass du mit dem Rauchen aufhörst.
6. Du kannst sie nicht zwingen, Dolmetscherin zu werden, wenn sie nicht will.
7. Ich dachte immer, dass er ein ehrlicher Mann sei.
8. Er sagte mir, dass ich an den Erfolg glauben sollte.
9. Er erlaubte uns nicht, die Wunderdroge auszuprobieren.
10. Ich muss mich erinnnern, dass ich Blumen kaufe.
11. Sie überredete uns, das Basketballspielen aufzugeben.
12. Ich denke, dass sie sehr freundlich ist.
13. Ich möchte nicht, dass du so viel süßes Zeug isst.
14. Er erklärte wie man Brot bäckt.
15. Er bat mich, den Abfall wegzuwerfen.
16. Ich möchte, dass er heimkommt.
17. Er mag nicht, dass wir zu spät kommen.
18. Bitte, zeig mir, wie ich den Tennisschläger schwingen muss.
19. Bitte erinnere mich, dass ich den Fernseher leiser stelle.
20. Er überredete sie, dass sie Vegetarierin wird.
21. Wir sahen ihn betrunken nach Hause kommen.
22. Könnten Sie mir helfen, das Paket zu tragen?
23. Er veranlasste uns, hart für den Wettbewerb zu trainieren.
24. Wir schlugen ihr vor, über Nacht bei uns zu bleiben.
25. Du bringst uns immer zum Lachen.
26. Wir wurden nicht gehört, als wir sangen.
27. Er wurde in Ruhe gelassen, nachdem er die Rechnung bezahlt hatte.
28. Ich mag nicht, wenn du / dass du eine große Menge Schlagobers nimmst.
29. Ich sagte ihm, wann wir uns treffen.
30. Sie weiß nie, was sie sagen soll.
31. Er ist sich nicht sicher, welche Hose er anziehen soll.
32. Er sagte uns nicht, wen wir einladen sollen.
33. Fred sagt ihr immer, was sie denken und tun soll.
34. Kannst du mir sagen, wo ich meinen Schirm suchen soll?
35. Ich möchte, dass sie Französisch lernt.
36. Ich schlug ihm vor, dass er mein Auto nimmt.

THE PASSIVE INFINITIVE

The passive infinitive is used **when the doer is not mentioned.**
(wenn der Handelnde nicht genannt ist)

> 1. after for example **want, be (is, am, are, was, were),**
>   **remain, leave**

He wants **to be left** alone now.
She is **to be seen** in the local newspaper.
(Man kann sie in der Lokalzeitung sehen.)
You are **to be pitied**. (Du bist zu bemitleiden.)
The key was not **to be found**. (Der Schlüssel konnte nicht gefunden werden.)
To be sold. (Zu verkaufen.)
This house is not **to be sold**.
It remains **to be asked**. (Das bleibt noch zu fragen.)
His behaviour leaves a lot **to be desired**.
(Sein Benehmen lässt sehr zu wünschen übrig.)

> 2. after **modal verbs:** **must, shall, should, have to,**
>   **ought to, mustn't, can, can't,**
>   **will, would, may, might ...**

Attention: with **modal verbs** use the infinitive **without to**
(except for: ought to, have to)

Some work must **be done** in the garden.
She ought to **be helped**.
He should **be told** the truth.
Her room had to **be cleaned** after the party.
The cat must **be fed**.
These flowers mustn't **be picked**.
Her book will **be published** in May.
The meal must **be cooked** now.
The dog should **be taken** for a walk.
His pictures can **be seen** in the museum.
This riddle can't **be solved**.
The pop concert could **be heard** in the whole town.

3. In many cases both **active and passive** infinitive **is possible**:

(In vielen Fällen ist sowohl der aktive als auch der passive Infinitiv möglich.)

a) after: **there is**

There is a bill **to pay**.	=	**to be paid**.
There is no time **to lose**.	=	**to be lost**.
There is no more **to say**.	=	**to be said**.

Ein kleiner Bedeutungsunterschied besteht:

There is nothing **to do**.
(Es gibt nichts zu tun, keine Unterhaltungsmöglichkeit.)
There is nothing **to be done**.
(Es gibt nichts, was man hätte tun können. Es ist vorbei.)

b) after: *two* adjectives (for example after: **too** and **enough**)

The soup is too hot **to eat**.	=	**to be eaten**.
The suitcase is too heavy **to carry**.	=	**to be carried**.
This milk isn't good enough **to drink**.	=	**to be drunk**.
The cheese isn't fresh enough **to eat**.	=	**to be eaten**.

4. ATTENTION: You normally use the **active infinitive**

a) after: *one* adjective

This book is <u>easy</u> **to read**.
Fresh milk is <u>fine</u> **to drink**.
The Easter eggs were <u>difficult</u> **to find**.
The baby is <u>lovely</u> **to look at**.
The grammar rules are <u>easy</u> **to explain**.
This film is <u>interesting</u> **to watch**.
Lunch is <u>ready</u> **to eat**!
The window is <u>difficult</u> **to open**.

b) after: too, enough + *for me / you / him / her / us / them*

The film is **too terrible** *for me* **to watch**.
This book is **too trashy** *for her* **to read**.
He is **too impolite** *for me* **to talk to**.
The soup is **too salty** *for him* **to eat**.
This pop band is **too loud** *for me* **to listen to**.
The exam is **easy enough** *for him* **to pass**.
This meal is **tasty enough** *for her* **to eat**.
This water isn't **cold enough** *for me* **to drink**.

c) after: **article + adjective + noun**

This is *an easy question* **to answer**.
He is *a charming man* **to talk to**.
This is *a terrible film* **to watch**.
This is *an awful song* **to listen to**.

d) in the following expressions:

Rooms **to let**.
There are rooms **to let** near the university.
There is a house **to let** in Apron Road.

PASSIVE OR ACTIVE INFINITIVE

1. The dog must .... (take) for a walk.
2. The crossword puzzle can't .... (solve).
3. These three letters must .... (write) by Friday.
4. This book is funny to .... (read).
5. I'm not to .... (blame). It's all your fault.
6. Many questions remain to .... (answer).
7. This picture is not to .... (sell). It belongs to Mr Swan.
8. There is much work to .... (do).
9. This cheese isn't fresh enough to .... (eat).
10. This cheese isn't fresh enough for me to .... (eat).
11. Letters of complaint can .... (send) to the city authority.
12. His keys might .... (steal).
13. The composition is to .... (write) by Monday.
14. The coffee is too hot to .... (drink).
15. The bill should .... (pay) by March 10th.
16. Her cries could .... (hear) down the road.
17. The homework must .... (hand) in on Tuesday.
18. Bello ought to .... (give) his bone. He is hungry.
19. Poor Mr Frank is to .... (pity).
20. Her last thriller leaves much to .... (desire).
21. This awful CD can't .... (listen) to.
22. Did you see the sign "To .... (sell)"?
23. There is still much that remains to .... (do).
24. In King's Road there are lots of rooms to .... (let).
25. This exam is too difficult for him to .... (pass).
26. This exam is too difficult to .... (pass).
27. This exam is difficult to .... (pass).
28. This charming girl must .... (love).
29. Sue doesn't want to .... (leave) alone at night.
30. If she goes on like this she might .... (fire).
31. This exciting book must .... (read).
32. This restaurant will .... (open) in March.
33. He wants to .... (leave) alone now.
34. The windows ought to .... (clean).
35. Unfortunately his problems can't .... (solve).
36. This lovely child must .... (kiss).
37. She hopes to .... (invite) to his party.
38. These flowers mustn't .... (pick).
39. A lot of things remain to .... (talk) about.

40. This is horrible handwriting to .... (read).
41. Cold water is refreshing to .... (drink).
42. The shopping centre is easy to .... (reach).
43. The shopping centre is easy enough to .... (reach).
44. The shopping centre is easy enough for us to .... (reach).
45. This new pen is super to .... (write) with.
46. He is too dull to .... (invite).
47. He is too dull for us to .... (invite).
48. There is a letter to .... (answer).
49. She ought to .... (tell) the whole truth.
50. My purse was not to .... (find).
51. His vintage car is not to .... (sell).
52. There is nothing to .... (do).
53. Bob can't .... (take) to the restaurant because he slurps.
54. Sour milk is awful to .... (smell).
55. His table manners leave much to .... (desire).
56. The cream ought to .... (put) into the fridge.
57. This question is difficult to .... (answer).
58. This question is too difficult to .... (answer).
59. This question is too difficult for me to .... (answer).
60. He wants to .... (leave) alone.
61. Your socks have to .... (mend).
62. This view is marvellous to .... (look) at.
63. The soup is too salty to .... (eat).
64. Hurry up! There is no time to .... (lose).
65. This film is not easy to .... (understand).
66. The cupboard is too heavy to .... (carry).
67. The cupboard is too heavy for us to .... (carry).
68. The cupboard is heavy to .... (carry).
69. After our walk my shoes had to .... (clean).
70. He is an impolite person to .... (talk) to.
71. Tea is ready to .... (drink).
72. This apple is not ripe enough to .... (eat).
73. My new bike is great to .... (ride) with.
74. All kinds of books are to .... (find) in the library.
75. He is always the first to .... (see) at a party.
76. Suddenly the child was not to .... (see) any more.
77. In the new housing estate many flats are to .... (sell).
78. There is still something to .... (do) about his bad mark.
79. Your teacher must .... (ask) about it.

GERMAN „MAN"

Man sagt ...

They say that she is a very charming woman.
People say that she is a very charming woman.
It is said that she is a very charming woman.
She is said to be a very charming woman.

Man sagte ...

They said that Mr Jones was very rich.
People said that Mr Jones was very rich.
It was said that Mr Jones was very rich.
Mr Jones was said to be very rich.

Man denkt ...

They think that Linda is having a baby.
People think that Linda is having a baby.
It is thought that Linda is having a baby.
Linda is thought to be having a baby.

Man dachte ...

They thought that the Millers had sold their house.
People thought that the Millers had sold their house.
It was thought that the Millers had sold their house.
The Millers were thought to have sold their house.

Man weiß ...

They know that Mrs Smith is divorced.
People know that Mrs Smith is divorced.
It is known that Mrs Smith is divorced.
Mrs Smith is known to be divorced.

Man wusste ...

They knew that Frank had gone to Canada.
People knew that Frank had gone to Canada.
It was known that Frank had gone to Canada.
Frank was known to have gone to Canada.

Man vermutet ...

They suppose that he is somewhere in America.
People suppose that he is somewhere in America.
It is supposed that he is somewhere in America.
He is supposed to be somewhere in America.

Man vermutete ...

They supposed that he had been in prison.
People supposed that he had been in prison.
It was supposed that he had been in prison.
He was supposed to be the candidate for the next election.

Constructions of that kind are also possible with:

find	*(be)finden*
claim	*behaupten*
report	*berichten*
believe	*glauben*
consider*	*in Betracht ziehen*
understand*	*verstehen*

* Also see GERUND p 63 f

TRANSLATE GERMAN „MAN" CONSTRUCTIONS

1. Man sagt, dass sie sich ein Zimmer teilen.
2. Man vermutet, dass Herr Schneider sehr reich ist.
3. Man glaubt, dass Frau Miller an ihrem Mann herumnörgelt.
4. Man dachte, dass er zurückkommen würde.
5. Man fand, dass er sehr eigenartig war.
6. Man berichtet, dass sie im Lotto gewonnen hat.
7. Man weiß, dass er seinen Vater bei einem Bootsunfall verloren hat.
8. Man dachte nicht, dass er ihr helfen würde.
9. Man vermutet, dass es in dem Haus spukt.
10. Man zog in Betracht, dass man ihn am Freitag besuchen könnte.
11. Man sagt, dass er ein sehr freundlicher Lehrer ist.
12. Man denkt, dass Herr Stone sein Auto verkaufen wird.
13. Man vermutete, dass er davonlaufen würde.
14. Man weiß, dass er sich ein Haus kauft.
15. Man glaubt, dass sie geschieden sind.
16. Man berichtete, dass er den ersten Preis gewonnen hatte.
17. Man glaubt, dass das Haus im 16. Jahrhundert gebaut wurde.
18. Man dachte nicht, dass das Mädchen noch am Leben war.
19. Man vermutete, dass er nicht da sein würde.
20. Man behauptete, dass er sehr eifersüchtig war.
21. Man denkt, dass Shi Xuxi der älteste Mann der Welt ist.
22. Man berichtet, dass der Krieg vorüber ist.
23. Man behauptet, dass er ein guter Vater ist.
24. Man berichtet, dass der gestohlene Ring mehr als 5000 Pfund wert ist.
25. Man glaubte nicht, dass er so schnell laufen konnte.
26. Man sagt, dass „Schindlers Liste" einer der besten Filme von Spielberg ist.
27. Man sagte, dass er Kinder sehr gern hatte.
28. Man fand nicht, dass die Prüfung schwierig war.
29. Man dachte, dass Maria ihren Mann in Wien kennengelernt hatte.
30. Man sagt, dass er eine neue Freundin hat.
31. Man weiß, dass Charly gerne kocht.
32. Man vermutete, dass er das Geld gestohlen hatte.
33. Man denkt, dass Laura krank war.
34. Man behauptet, dass Herr Jones im Spital ist.
35. Man berichtete, dass er sehr traurig war.
36. Man berichtete, dass das Schiff vermisst wird.
37. Man versteht, dass er so aufgeregt ist.
38. Man vermutet, dass er bald heiraten wird.
39. Man wusste, dass er nicht lange bleiben würde.
40. Man sagte, dass Frank lange in Amerika gewesen war.

THE PERFECT INFINITIVE

1. with *to*
   after: **seem, appear, pretend** *(vortäuschen)*, **ought** *(eigentlich sollen)*

He seems **to have seen** her before.
(Er scheint sie früher schon gesehen zu haben.)
He appears **to have met** her some day.
(Er scheint sie irgendwann getroffen zu haben.)
He pretended **to have read** the book.
(Er tat, als ob er ... gelesen hätte.)
He ought **to have helped** her.
(Er hätte ihr eigentlich helfen sollen.)

2. without *to*:
   after: **may, might, must, can, can't, could, needn't, should, would**

We may **have seen** them.
I must **have been** there before.
I should **have told** him.
He can't **have lifted** the stone alone.
He would **have been** happy to see her.
He could **have managed**.
They needn't **have hurried**.
She might **have found** the mistake.

THE CONTINUOUS INFINITIVE

I. PRESENT CONTINUOUS:

1. with *to*

after: **seem, appear, pretend** *(vortäuschen)*, **ought** *(eigentlich sollen)*

She seems **to be waiting** for someone.
He appears **to be working**.
She pretends **to be sleeping**.
She ought **to be working** now. *(Sie sollte jetzt eigentlich arbeiten.)*

2. without *to*:

after: **may, might, must, can, can't, could, needn't, should, would**

You shouldn't **be smoking**.
She might **be working** now.
She may **be sleeping** at present.
She must **be working** in the garden now.

II. PERFECT CONTINUOUS:

1. with *to*

after: **seem, appear, pretend** *(vortäuschen)*, **ought** *(eigentlich sollen)*

She seems **to have been waiting** for someone.
He appears **to have been working**.
She pretends **to have been sleeping**.
She ought **to have been working**.

2. without *to*:

after: **may, might, must, can, can't, could, needn't, should, would**

You shouldn't **have been smoking**.
She might **have been working** up to now.
She may **have been sleeping**.
She must **have been working** in the garden.

III. FUTURE CONTINUOUS: without *to* after **will**

I will **be working** from nine to five tomorrow.
He will **be sleeping** the whole afternoon.

THE GERUND

The GERUND is an **ing-form** and can be used in the **active** and the **passive** form.

	active	passive
Present	seeing	being seen
Perfect	having seen	having been seen

1. It is used as a **verbal noun** *(hauptwörtlich gebrauchtes Zeitwort)* **with** or **without** an article

Examples:
    Swimming is healthy.
    The smoking of cigarettes is unhealthy.
    Bungee jumping is dangerous.
    Reading thrillers is fun.
    No **smoking**!

2. It is used after **possessive adjectives** and **accusative personal pronouns**

Examples:
    Do you mind *my* **smoking**? (written, formal English)
    Do you mind *me* **smoking**? (spoken English)

    I can't stand *their* **complaining** all the time. (written, formal English)
    I can't stand *them* **complaining** all the time. (spoken English)

3. It is used after **possessive cases**

Examples:
    Mother doesn't like *the man's* **being** so impolite. (written, formal English)
    Mother doesn't like *the man* **being** so impolite. (spoken English)

    I hate *people's* **coughing** at concerts. (written, formal English)
    I hate *people* **coughing** at concerts. (spoken English)

    We must avoid *Peter's* **telling** the secret. (written, formal English)
    We must avoid *Peter* **telling** the secret. (spoken English)

4. It is used after **following verbs**

admit* *	zugeben	**involve**	beinhalten
advise*	raten, empfehlen	**keep**	immer wieder/ dauernd tun
allow*	erlauben	**like***	
anticipate	Vorwegnehmen	**love***	
appreciate	schätzen, anerkennen	**mention**	erwähnen
avoid	vermeiden	**mean***	
begin*		**mind**	ausmachen
consider	in Betracht ziehen	**miss**	verpassen, nicht schaffen
continue*	weitermachen	**need***	
delay	verschieben	**pardon**	verzeihen
deny* *	leugnen	**permit***	erlauben
detest*	ablehnen, hassen	**postpone**	verschieben
dislike*	nicht mögen	**practise**	üben
dread	fürchten	**prefer***	vorziehen
enjoy	gerne tun	**recollect**	sich erinnern
escape	entkommen	**regret*** *	bedauern
excuse	entschuldigen	**remember***	
fail	versagen, scheitern	**resent**	übelnehmen
fancy	sich vorstellen, einbilden	**resist**	widerstehen
finish	beenden	**risk**	riskieren
forbid	verbieten	**start***	
forget*	vergessen	**stop***	
forgive	vergeben	**suggest*** *	vorschlagen
hate*	hassen	**try***	
imagine	sich vorstellen	**understand**	
intend*	beabsichtigen	**want***	

* **Attention 1:** Also see pages 73 ff
** **Attention 2:** Words like *admit, deny, regret, suggest* may be followed by a – **that clause**.
She denied **that** she had told him the secret. =
She denied **telling** him the secret. =
She denied **having told** him the secret.

Examples:

I am *considering* going to France.
Ich ziehe es in Betracht, nach Frankreich zu gehen.
He *missed* winning the first prize.
Er schaffte es nicht, den ersten Preis zu gewinnen.
Please *pardon* my mentioning it.
Bitte verzeih, dass ich es erwähnt habe.
Does his job *involve* using the computer?
Beinhaltet sein Beruf die Verwendung eines Computers?
Keep smiling!
Immer nur lächeln!
She *keeps* talking about her children all the time.
Sie redet dauernd über ihre Kinder.
Please *excuse* my interrupting you.
Bitte entschuldige, dass ich dich unterbreche.
Our neighbours are *considering* building a house.
Unsere Nachbarn ziehen es in Betracht, ein Haus zu bauen.
He doesn't *mind* taking the dog for a walk.
Es macht ihm nichts aus, mit dem Hund spazieren zu gehen.
He *admitted* stealing the money.
Er gab zu, das Geld gestohlen zu haben.
Fancy meeting the girl of your dreams!
Stell dir vor, dass du dein Traummädchen triffst.
He *hates* being made fun of.
Er hasst es, ausgelacht zu werden.
Father *forbade* us going to the cinema.
Vater verbat uns, ins Kino zu gehen.
We should *postpone* travelling abroad.
Wir sollten die Reise ins Ausland verschieben.
We mustn't *risk* being seen.
Wir dürfen es nicht riskieren, gesehen zu werden.
Please don't *mention* meeting Bill last night.
Bitte erwähne es nicht, dass du Bill gestern Nacht getroffen hast.

5. It is used after **verbs + prepositions**

accuse of anklagen, beschuldigen	**escape from** entkommen
adjust to anpassen an	**forget about** vergessen
agree with zustimmen	**forgive for** verzeihen
aim at abzielen auf	**give up** aufhören
apologize for sich entschuldigen	**go on** weiter machen
approve of dafür sein	**insist on** darauf bestehen
ask about sich erkundigen nach	**keep on** immer wieder / dauernd tun
ask for fragen nach, bitten um	**leave off** aufhören, ablassen
be against dagegen sein	**look forward to** sich freuen auf
be for dafür sein	**negotiate about** verhandeln über
begin by beginnen mit	**object to** dagegen sein
believe in glauben an	**prevent from** daran hindern
benefit from profitieren	**protect from** davor schützen
blame for tadeln	**put off** aufschieben
boast of prahlen wegen	**refrain from** unterlassen
care for sich kümmern um	**rely on** sich darauf verlassen
carry on weitermachen	**save from** davor bewahren
charge with belasten, vorwerfen	**see about** sich kümmern um
complain of beklagen	**speak about** darüber sprechen
concentrate on konzentrieren auf	**speak of** davon sprechen
confess to sich bekennen zu, zugeben	**specialize in** sich spezialisieren
congratulate on gratulieren zu	**spend on** ausgeben für
consist of bestehen aus	**stop (from)** abhalten von
cope with fertig werden mit	**succeed in** Erfolg haben
count on darauf zählen	**suspect of** verdächtigen
decide against gegen etw. entscheiden	**take to** beginnen
decide for/on für etwas entscheiden	**take part in** teilnehmen an
delight in sich daran erfreuen	**talk about** darüber sprechen
depend on abhängen von	**talk somebody into** überreden
despair of daran verzweifeln	**thank for** danken für
devote to widmen	**think of/about** daran denken
die of sterben an	**vote against** dagegenstimmen
disapprove of dagegen sein	**warn against** davor warnen
dream of davon träumen	**worry about** sich Sorgen machen

Examples:
She *complains of* **not having** enough money.
He *took to* **drinking after** his wife's death.
They *stopped* the man (*from*) **entering** the building.
He always *spoke of* **going** to America.

6. It is used after **adjectives + prepositions**

accustomed to *gewohnt sein*	**happy at** *glücklich sein über*
afraid of *sich fürchten vor*	**impressed by** *beeindruckt von*
alarmed at *bestürzt, beängstigt*	**interested in** *interessiert sein an*
angry at/about *zornig sein*	**involved in** *verwickelt sein in*
annoyed at/about *verärgert sein*	**keen on** *gern haben*
appropriate for *geeignet für*	**pleased at/about** *erfreut sein*
astonished at *erstaunt sein*	**proud of** *stolz sein wegen*
bad at/in *schlecht sein bei*	**ready for** *bereit sein zu*
capable of *fähig sein*	**right in/about** *Recht haben*
certain of *sicher sein*	**sad about/at** *traurig sein über*
charged with *angeklagt wegen*	**shocked about/at** *schockiert sein*
clever at *geschickt, klug sein*	**sick of** *es satt haben*
crazy about *verrückt nach*	to be/feel **sorry for/about**
conscious of *bewusst sein*	**sure about** *sicher sein wegen*
delighted about *erfreut sein über*	**surprised at** *erstaunt sein*
disappointed at *enttäuscht sein*	**tired from** *müde sein von*
excited about *aufgeregt, begeistert*	to be **tired of** *es satt haben*
famous for *berühmt sein für*	to grow **tired of** *die Lust verlieren an*
far from *weit entfernt sein von*	**thankful for** *dankbar sein für*
fed up with *es satt haben*	**used for** *verwendet werden für*
fined for *Geldstrafe bekommen*	**used to** *gewöhnt sein an*
fond of *begeistert sein, gerne tun*	to get **used to** *sich an etwas gewöhnen*
free from *frei sein*	**worried about** *sich Sorgen machen*
glad at/about *froh sein über*	**wrong in** *Unrecht haben*
good at *gut sein bei/ in*	

Examples:

***Sorry for** being* late.

Entschuldigung, dass ich zu spät komme.

You are ***wrong in** thinking* that she is arrogant.

Du irrst, wenn du meinst, dass sie arrogant ist.

He was ***charged with** driving* too fast.

Er wurde wegen Zuschnellfahrens angeklagt.

I am ***used to** working* late at night.

Ich bin es gewöhnt, spät in der Nacht zu arbeiten.

She is ***tired from** staying up* late.

Sie ist müde vom langen Aufbleiben.

7. It is used after **nouns + prepositions**

advantage of Vorteil	**gift of** die Begabung für/zu
alternative of Alternative zu	**idea of** Idee, Ahnung, Plan
art to / in / of Kunst	**opportunity of*** Gelegenheit zu
aversion to Abneigung gegen	<u>the</u> **point (of)** Zweck, Sinn, Begriff
chance of*	<u>no</u> **point (in)** keinen Sinn haben
choice between Wahl zwischen	**reason for** Grund für
danger of Gefahr	take **interest in** Interesse haben für
difficulty (in) Schwierigkeit bei	**trouble (in)** Schwierigkeit bei
doubt about Zweifel an	**way of** Art und Weise
experience in Erfahrung in	**freedom of**
mood for Stimmung zu	**possibility of / for*** Möglichkeit

* **Gerund** as well as **infinitive** are possible:

They have a **chance of winning** the World Cup. *(Chance)*
I haven't had a **chance to meet** him yet. *(Gelegenheit)*

She has the **opportunity of going** / **to go** abroad in her summer holidays.
(Möglichkeit, Gelegenheit)

Examples:
There is no **possibility of influencing** him.	*Es gibt keine Möglichkeit, ihn zu beeinflussen.*
I don't see the **point of helping** him.	*Ich sehe keinen Sinn darin, ihm zu helfen.*
I'm on the **point of crying**.	*Ich bin im Begriff, zu weinen.*
There's no **point in staying** longer.	*Es hat keinen Sinn, länger zu bleiben.*
There's no **point quarrelling**.	*Es hat keinen Zweck, zu streiten.*
I don't like his **way of looking** at me.	*Ich mag nicht, wie er mich ansieht.*
We had **difficulty (in) finding** a cheap hotel.	*Wir hatten Schwierigkeiten, ein billiges Hotel zu finden.*
I'm not in the **mood for playing** right now.	*Ich bin jetzt nicht zum Spielen aufgelegt.*

8. It is used after **certain expressions**

can't stand/bear nicht ertragen können	**How about ...?** Wie wäre es mit ...?
can't help nicht anders können	**What about ...?** Wie wäre es mit ...?
it's worth wert sein	**there is no** man (kann) nicht
it is fun es macht Spaß	**this is** das bedeutet, das heißt
it's no good es hat keinen Sinn	**to be busy** beschäftigt sein
it's no use es nützt nichts	**to feel like** zumute sein nach
It's a waste of time/money	**Thank you for**
to waste (one's) time/money Zeit/Geld verschwenden	

Examples:

He **can't help** crying.

Er kann nicht anders, er muss weinen.

It's no use crying now.

Es nützt nichts, jetzt zu weinen.

Is this film **worth** seeing?

Ist es der Film wert, gesehen zu werden?

It is fun having a party.

Eine Party zu haben macht Spaß.

It's no good telling him about it.

Es ist nicht gut / hat keinen Sinn, ihm davon zu erzählen.

On the telephone: **This is** Sue speaking.

Hier spricht Sue.

That is asking too much!

Das ist zu viel verlangt!

He is **busy** cleaning the windows.

Er ist mit Fenster putzen beschäftigt.

I don't **feel like** going for a walk now.

Mir ist jetzt nicht nach einem Spaziergang zumute.

Thank you for being so kind.

Danke, dass du so nett bist/warst.

You didn't **waste much time** getting here!

Du hast dich aber sehr beeilt, um herzukommen!

You are **wasting your time** talking to him.

Du vergeudest deine Zeit, wenn du mit ihm sprichst.

There is no knowing where he will go next.

Man weiß nicht, wo er als Nächstes hingehen wird.

I **can't stand** being shouted at.

Ich kann es nicht ertragen, wenn man mich anschreit.

How about going to London this year?

Wie wäre es, wenn wir heuer nach London fahren?

FILL IN GERUND AND PREPOSITIONS

1. Mr Racer was accused .... (drive) too fast.
2. I'm looking forward .... (spend) my holidays in Ireland.
3. He was rather astonished .... (meet) her at Blarney Castle.
4. Mr Smith gave .... (smoke) last winter.
5. Paul is crazy .... (eat) pizza.
6. Please think .... (buy) a road map.
7. He insisted .... (visit) a singing pub.
8. Tom was annoyed .... (not find) his cap.
9. I'm really tired .... (listen to) all that good advice.
10. She is fond .... (drive) her new car.
11. I'm keen .... (work) with children.
12. She was clever .... (not quarrel) with her friend.
13. We must vote .... (he / become) our coach.
14. Let's warn her .... (smoke) so much.
15. They all object .... (he / flirt) with young girls.
16. I've got difficulty .... (talk) with Jim.
17. Mr Anderson is famous .... (bake) wonderful cakes.
18. Mandy is not used .... (work) hard.
19. There's no point .... (complain).
20. I'm really sorry .... (not call) you yesterday.
21. She will never get used .... (get) up at six o'clock.
22. He has no trouble .... (keep) a secret.
23. Her charming way .... (treat) her pupils is to be admired.
24. The teacher was pleased .... (the pupils / prepare) so well for the test.
25. Is there a danger .... (fall) down the rock when you kiss the Blarney Stone?
26. Roger enjoys the freedom .... (travel) with his Interrail Pass.
27. My doubt .... (he / be) innocent is enormous.
28. His mouth trembled and he was on the point .... (cry).
29. She is very proud .... (win) the first prize.
30. I'm glad .... (meet) you here.
31. Mum is worried .... (he / behave) so badly.
32. You really have no reason .... (complain)!
33. We congratulated Chris .... (win) the tennis match.
34. She was excited .... (visit) the Ring of Kerry.
35. We had difficulty .... (find) a nice restaurant.

36. Mrs Sweet took .... (drink) because she was desperate.
37. Do you know the reason .... (she / leave) him?
38. Mum is tired .... (work) all day.
39. I'd like to apologize .... (be) late.
40. Mary must cope .... (be) alone in her holidays.
41. Let's forget .... (quarrel).
42. Please concentrate .... (work) carefully.
43. She is delighted .... (be) invited to their party.
44. I haven't got any experience .... (sail).
45. She was surprised .... (not meet) Linda at the concert.
46. He always succeeds .... (escape) the police.
47. You can rely .... (I / be) in front of the theatre at half past seven.
48. His parents couldn't prevent him .... (leave) his job.
49. Tommy is very good .... (climb) trees.
50. In spite .... (be) ill our teacher went to school.
51. Do you think he is capable .... (help) her?
52. I'm fond .... (have) a cup of tea in the afternoon.
53. We were talking .... (go) to America this year.
54. The thief finally confessed .... (steal) the ring.
55. Her children are not accustomed .... (do) that kind of work.
56. He always boasts .... (have) rich parents.
57. He has been offered an opportunity .... (work) in Germany for one year.
58. You are wrong .... (think) that you can trust him.
59. Did you have any difficulty .... (find) her new address?
60. My parents don't approve .... (I / stay) out late at night.
61. Why does he think .... (move) to Vienna?
62. I'm far .... (believe) his lies.
63. She takes no interest .... (make) friends with her new neighbours.
64. If there is any danger .... (meet) him at Joe's birthday party, I'm not going.
65. I'm sure you are capable .... (do) much better than you did yesterday.
66. I'm not interested .... (listen) to his old stories.
67. Am I right .... (think) that we met at Mr Fisher's barbecue three weeks ago?

68. He is conscious .... (be) old enough to decide on his own.
69. She objects .... (he / spend) all his money on cars.
70. Father insists .... (she / not drive) too fast because he's afraid .... (she / damage) his car.
71. Poor Nancy has a lot of trouble .... (get) a good job.
72. Let's take the advantage .... (book) our seats in advance! We might get better ones.
73. There's a special art .... (know) when to give up.
74. I'm really sad .... (he / be) ill.
75. Sue was impressed .... (Mr Miller / be) such a gentleman.
76. What's the point .... (try)?
77. I feel sorry .... (forget) your birthday.
78. He has a deep aversion .... (walk) in the rain.
79. Her husband is very clever .... (handle) all kinds of machines.
80. She is fed .... (work) late at night.
81. I was so pleased .... (he / bring) me a wonderful bunch of flowers.
82. There must be an alternative .... (go) to a bar every night.
83. You can count .... (I / help) you tomorrow.
84. Leave .... (tease) your little sister!
85. I'm really thankful .... (you / help) me so fast.
86. He despairs .... (she / drink) too much at parties.
87. He should devote his time .... (read) good books.
88. Let's begin .... (mow) the grass.
89. The teacher blamed him .... (throw) stones at Billy.
90. We'll have to make a choice .... (go) to the Chinese or to the pizzeria.
91. I admire Ben. He's got the gift .... (talk).
92. My reason .... (leave) earlier was my terrible headache.
93. He was on the point .... (tell) me the secret, when suddenly the telephone rang.
94. Lucy had the idea .... (start) a tea-house.
95. She has always dreamed .... (drive) a fast car.
96. The teacher insists .... (we / do) our homework carefully.
97. I'm looking forward .... (visit) the Cliffs of Moher.
98. She must cope .... (care) for three little children.
99. Go .... (talk). I don't want to disturb you.

GERUND OR INFINITIVE

Either infinitive or **gerund** may be used after:

(Entweder Gerund oder Infinitiv können verwendet werden nach:)

1. begin, start, continue, intend *(beabsichtigen)*

Gerund or **infinitive** may be used **without any difference in meaning**.
(Gerund oder Infinitiv können ohne Bedeutungsunterschied verwendet werden.)

Examples: Please *begin* working.   = Please *begin* to work.
            He *starts* singing.   = He *starts* to sing.
            She *intends* having a party. = She *intends* to have a party.

Attention: If the verb following **begin, start, continue** is a verb of **knowing** and **understanding**, the **infinitive** must be used.
(Wenn das Verb, das begin, start, continue folgt, ein Verb des Wissens und Verstehens ist, muss der Infinitiv verwendet werden.)

Examples: We *began* to understand.
            We *began* to see what he wanted.
            (Wir begannen zu begreifen, was er wollte.)

2. love, like, dislike, detest, hate, can't bear, prefer, allow, permit, forbid, advise

The **gerund** is used in a **general** situation, for expressing a **general** statement. *(für eine allgemeine Situation, um eine generelle Aussage zu machen).*
The **infinitive** is used in a **specific** situation.

General: He *hates* waiting for the bus as a rule.
            In der Regel hasst er es, auf den Bus zu warten.
            He doesn't *like* drinking alcohol.
            He *prefers* hiking to biking.
            She *can't bear* being at home alone.
            We don't *allow* smoking in the living room.
            They *forbid* walking on the grass.
            They *advise* leaving the suitcases outside.
            (Man rät, die Koffer draußen zu lassen.)

Specific: He *hates* **to wait** today because it is raining.
I really *hate* **to go** now, but I have to.
He wouldn't *like* **to drink** alcohol today because he is feeling sick.
I *prefer* **to walk** today morning, because the weather is fine.
She *can't bear* **to be** alone tonight.
Would you *like* **to stay** here? (specific situation with would)
Would you *prefer* **to have** a cup of tea?
He'd *hate* **to spend** all his life in a big town.
I'd *love* **to see** you tomorrow.
Mother doesn't *allow* Fred **to stay** out after midnight.
(Specific situation because the person is mentioned.)
(also see: OBJECT WITH THE INFINITIVE p 46 ff)
Father *forbids* us **to go** to the cinema.
She *advised* Tom **to be** back by eight.

3. remember, forget, regret	
Gerund:	You remember, regret or forget an action in **the past**. Remembering, regretting, forgetting is the second action.
Infinitive:	Is used for an action referring to **the future**. Remembering, regretting, forgetting is the first action. (Im Deutschen steht oft „müssen".)

Examples:
I *remember* **meeting** her in the supermarket.
(Ich erinnere mich, dass ich sie im Supermarkt getroffen habe. – vergangen)
(Erinnern ist die zweite Handlung, das Treffen die erste.)
Please *remember* **to post** the letter for me.
(Bitte, erinnere dich daran, dass du den Brief für mich aufgeben musst. –
Brief aufgeben liegt in der Zukunft)
(Erinnern ist die erste Handlung, Briefaufgeben die zweite.)
I must *remember* **to inform** him.
(Ich muss mich daran erinnern, dass ich ihn informieren muss. – Zukunft)
(Erinnern ist die erste Handlung, Informieren die zweite.)
Please *remember* **to hand** in your homework.
(Bitte erinnert euch, dass ihr die Hausübungen abgeben müsst. – Zukunft)
(Erinnern ist die erste Handlung, Hausübung abgeben die zweite.)
I'll never *forget* **seeing** "The Picture of Dorian Gray".
(Ich werde nie vergessen, dass ich den Film ... gesehen habe. – vergangen)
(Vergessen ist die zweite Handlung, das Filmsehen die erste.)
Please don't *forget* **to water** the flowers on Friday.
(Bitte vergiss nicht, die Blumen am Freitag zu gießen. – Zukunft)

I *regret* **saying** this to you.

(Ich bedaure, das zu dir gesagt zu haben. – <u>vergangen</u>)

(Bedauern ist die zweite Handlung, das Sagen die erste.)

I *regret* **to say** that he hasn't arrived yet.

(Ich bedaure, sagen zu <u>müssen</u> ...)

(Bedauern ist die erste Handlung, Sagen die zweite.)

I *regret* **to tell** you the truth about him.

(... dass ich dir sagen <u>muss</u> ...)

I *regret* **telling** you the secret.

(Ich bedaure, dir das Geheimnis gesagt zu haben. – <u>vergangen</u>)

4. mean

mean + Gerund	=	bedeuten
mean + infinitive	=	beabsichtigen, wollen

Examples:

If we want to catch the train, that will *mean* **leaving** at seven.

(... das <u>bedeutet</u>, dass wir um sieben weg müssen.)

Your bad mark *means* **working** harder next time.

(... <u>bedeutet</u>, dass du nächstes Mal ...)

I didn't *mean* **to hurt** him.

(Ich <u>wollte</u> ihn nicht verletzen.)

She never *meant* him **to find** out.

(Sie <u>hat</u> nie <u>gewollt</u>, dass er es herausfindet.)

I've been *meaning* **to write** to you for over two weeks.

(Ich <u>beabsichtige</u> schon seit mehr als zwei Wochen, dir zu schreiben.)

5. need, want

Infinitive: I *need* **to go** to bed earlier. *(active)*
You *needn't* **water** the flowers.
I *want* **to be** back at eight.

Gerund: My coat *needs* **cleaning**. *(passive) (British English)*
(Mein Mantel muss gereinigt werden.)
Your hair *wants* **cutting**. *(... muss geschnitten werden.) (British English)*
Our living room *wants* **painting**. *(... muss ausgemalt werden.) (British English)*

6. stop		
stop + gerund	=	stop an action *(aufhören)*
stop + infinitive	=	stehen bleiben; mit etwas aufhören, um etwas anderes zu tun

Examples:

She *stopped* singing.

(Sie hörte mit dem Singen auf.)

He *stopped* watching TV.

(Er hörte mit dem Fernsehen auf.)

I *stopped* to have a chat with my neighbour.

(Ich blieb stehen, um mit meinem Nachbarn zu plaudern.)

She *stopped* to have tea.

(Sie hörte mit etwas / mit einer anderen Arbeit auf, um Tee zu trinken.)

7. go on				
go on	+	gerund	=	mit einer Handlung weitermachen
go on	+	infinitive	=	und dann, als Nächstes

Examples:

I can't *go on* living like that, all that stress!

(Ich kann so nicht mehr weiterleben, dieser ganze Stress!)

She *went on* working although it was midnight.

(Sie arbeitete weiter, obwohl es Mitternacht war.)

She wants to *go on* being a teacher. / She wants to *keep on* teaching.

(Sie möchte Lehrerin bleiben.)

Go on speaking!

(Sprechen Sie weiter! / Sprich weiter!)

He *went on* to explain the facts.

(Und dann erklärte er die Fakten.)

She *went on* to say that she wanted to go to France.

(Und dann / Als Nächstes sagte sie ...)

8. try

try + gerund	=	**to make an experiment, a test** *(ausprobieren)*
try + infinitive	=	**to attempt** *(versuchen, sich bemühen)*

Examples:

***Try* throwing** a stone onto the window if I don't hear the bell.
(den Versuch machen, ausprobieren)
Have you ever ***tried* drinking** Coke with Retsina?
(den Versuch machen, ausprobieren)
She didn't understand German, so I ***tried* speaking** French to her.
(den Versuch machen, ausprobieren)

I ***tried* to sleep** but I couldn't. *(sich bemühen)*
Jack ***tried* to run** away, but his brother was faster. *(sich bemühen)*
She ***tried* to help** him. *(sich bemühen)*

GERUND OR INFINITIVE

Before doing this exercise revise the INFINITIVE pages 35 ff ... and OBJECT WITH THE INFINITIVE pages 46 ff.

1. He enjoys .... (have) a cup of tea in the afternoon.
2. Imagine .... (be) on a tropical island forever.
3. She hesitated .... (invite) him to her party.
4. Mary suggested .... (go) to the disco.
5. Fancy her .... (say) that to me!
6. He keeps .... (say) that he wants to spend his holidays in Ireland.
7. He doesn't mind .... (be) at a boarding school.
8. Imagine .... (go) for a day trip tomorrow.
9. Mary decided .... (go) to Canada this year.
10. Mary decided on .... (go) to Canada this year.
11. We happened .... (meet) him at the concert.
12. He is busy .... (do) his homework.
13. I resent her .... (shout) at me.
14. I won't risk .... (get) wet through and through.
15. I don't understand his .... (be) so impolite.
16. We had great difficulty (in) .... (find) a nice place for our picnic.
17. She was seen .... (give) Nick a kiss.
18. They warned us against .... (do) this again.
19. Please forgive my .... (make) fun of you.
20. Suddenly Ben began .... (understand).
21. She was disappointed at .... (find) the photo of another woman in his book.
22. We were disappointed .... (hear) that he had given up his job.
23. Mary intends .... (go) to Italy this year.
24. I don't feel like .... (work) now. I'm tired.
25. He couldn't help .... (tell) her that he loved her.
26. We watched the bird .... (make) a nest in the tree.
27. How about .... (visit) granny in the afternoon?
28. I can't prevent Charlie from .... (smoke).
29. I'd love .... (join) you but I have to stay.
30. You had better .... (leave) early, Bill.
31. Please remember .... (send) me a card from your holidays.
32. He managed .... (get) out of his car before it exploded.

33. Let me .... (give) you a piece of advice: .... (smoke) is dangerous.
34. Would you like .... (dance) this waltz with me?
35. I promise .... (pick) you up at seven.
36. I regret very much .... (hurt) you. I was so angry.
37. Stop .... (talk) please, I'd like .... (listen to) the news.
38. The frog tried .... (catch) the fly, but missed it.
39. I regret .... (tell) him this silly lie.
40. Fred likes .... (read) thrillers, but today he prefers .... (watch) TV.
41. Mary stopped at the fence.................. (talk) to Mrs Miller.
42. Fancy .... (be) a millionaire!
43. Mum always wants us .... (keep) our room tidy.
44. I don't mind your .... (listen) to the record now.
45. We watched the cat .... (catch) a mouse.
46. I hate your .... (make) such a terrible noise!
47. I must remember .... (tell) her that the flowers need .... (water).
48. She expects us .... (be) home for lunch at twelve.
49. The headmaster finished .... (speak) and we applauded.
50. You had better .... (take) the train at one o'clock.
51. Would you mind .... (tell) him that his idea is absolute nonsense?
52. I don't like .... (go) to the dentist's.
53. She wished .... (see) Ben again.
54. Imagine .... (lie) in the sun the whole afternoon.
55. He remembers .... (find) the purse in King's Street.
56. I hate .... (play) volleyball.
57. May I call a taxi for you? – No, thanks, I'd love .... (walk) now.
58. He always looks forward to .... (get) a present from his uncle.
59. It is time .... (go).
60. Try .... (drink) a glass of milk with honey. Your sore throat will soon be better.
61. My mother keeps .... (say) that I should be back by midnight.
62. Have you ever thought of .... (leave) your job?
63. He suddenly stopped .... (pick up) a coin.
64. Let's stop .... (visit) the church. There's an old painting inside that is worth .... (see).
65. His decision .... (go) was final.

66. Would you mind .... (turn) the radio off?
67. It's no use .... (ask) me again and again.
68. I can't stand your .... (interrupt) me all the time.
69. This awful horror film is not worth .... (see).
70. I told him my intention .... (go) to Paris.
71. He enjoys .... (flirt) with pretty girls.
72. I remember .... (look) briefly at the information.
73. I don't remember .... (fill) in the form.
74. Please don't mention .... (see) me in town yesterday.
75. Dad was ready .... (go), but mum kept him .... (wait).
76. The man admitted .... (steal) the money.
77. You haven't got the right .... (say) this.
78. You had better .... (leave) now before the guests arrive.
79. Let me .... (show) you how to use the instructions.
80. Mr Smith is proud of his son's .... (become) a lawyer.
81. He enjoys the freedom of .... (sleep) in a tent.
82. If you are fond of .... (fish), go to Canada.
83. Let's stop at the flower shop .... (get) some roses.
84. I wish I had practised .... (play) the recorder when I was young.
85. We got permission .... (leave) school at twelve.
86. I don't like .... (drink) beer at all.
87. I happened .... (meet) her in front of Big Ben. Imagine Sue .... (be) in London on her own!
88. Sorry about .... (disturb) you. – Never mind, we've just stopped .... (work).
89. I'm not in the mood .... (play) just now.
90. Please don't forget .... (write) a birthday card to your aunt.
91. I feel like .... (climb) this mountain tomorrow.
92. Her wish .... (leave) him is hard to understand.
93. They allowed us .... (spend) two weeks in their cottage in the mountains.
94. Please don't forget .... (explain) the way to me. Would you mind .... (bring) along your road map?
95. Our garden fence needs .... (paint) this summer.
96. I really don't remember .... (say) this to her.
97. Tom is always the first .... (fall) asleep.
98. Please don't forget .... (get) some bread on your way home!
99. He is angry at Linda's .... (use) his car without .... (ask).

100. It's no good .... (try) to persuade Jim .... (move) away from London.
101. You are always the only person .... (complain).
102. You are wrong in .... (think) that they will go for a compromise.
103. Most children are afraid of .... (be) left alone at night.
104. What a horrible place .... (spend) your night!
105. Stop .... (behave) like a fool!
106. I remember .... (pay) the bill on Friday.
107. I hate .... (get) up early in the morning.
108. Don't forget .... (wash) your hands before dinner.
109. She thinks her hair needs .... (dye) because there's a little bit of grey in it.
110. She regrets .... (give) him the money yesterday.
111. I wouldn't dare .... (ask) him now.
112. I don't allow him .... (smoke) his cigar in the house.
113. She is fed up with his .... (be) drunk every night.
114. What would you like .... (drink) now?
115. I hate Simon's .... (read) my letters.
116. Tom would sooner .... (ride) his bike than .... (practise) .... (playing) his recorder.
117. Liz hates his .... (read) the newspaper at breakfast.
118. Tim tried .... (help) us, but he couldn't.
119. I want him .... (get) some milk from the farmer.
120. We prefer .... (stay) at home to .... (go) to a party or a disco.
121. Don't you remember my .... (return) you your record last week?
122. Let's play a game! – No, thanks, I prefer .... (read) now.
123. I told him .... (stop) .... (smoke) because mother doesn't allow .... (smoke) in the living room.
124. Please stop .... (shout) like mad!
125. Father doesn't allow the boys .... (climb) the old tree because the branches might break.
126. I can't stand her .... (laugh) all the time.
127. She said she would love .... (go) to the Chinese restaurant on Saturday.
128. They don't allow .... (have) barbecues in the park.
129. She permitted us .... (stay) out after midnight.

130. Come and have a chat tonight! – Not tonight, I prefer.................................. (stay) at home.
131. Father doesn't like us .... (be) late.
132. I hate .... (tell) you the truth, but I must do so now.
133. My carpets want .... (hoover).
134. She hates him .... (leave) so early tonight.
135. She regrets .... (say) that he is a liar.
136. Tommy likes .... (knit).
137. We couldn't persuade him .... (stay) over the weekend.
138. I didn't mean .... (hurt) you, I didn't want .... (make) you .... (cry).
139. He took a walk with his dog, then he stopped .... (have) a chat with Mr Simons, his neighbour.
140. Tom, a left-hander, tried .... (write) with his right hand. He didn't succeed in .... (write) one single word legibly.
141. The teacher forbids us .... (eat) during the lesson.
142. Don't force me .... (call) the police!
143. John is unhappy at Doris .... (leave) him.
144. Try .... (persuade) him .... (give up) .... (smoke).
145. She regrets .... (move) to America last year.
146. She really hates .... (forget) him, but she must.
147. I'm afraid I forgot .... (call) Ben. I must do it now.
148. I dislike .... (watch) thrillers all alone. I'm afraid of .... (have) nightmares afterwards.
149. Would you like .... (have) lunch at twelve or later?
150. We heard them .... (whisper) in their room.
151. She stopped .... (work) because she nearly fell asleep.
152. Mother forbids us .... (eat) an ice cream before lunch.
153. He was seen .... (come) home wet through and through.
154. I love .... (have) a nice cup of tea in the morning.
155. My watch is broken! – No, its battery needs .... (change)!
156. The boys were observed .... (steal) the pears.
157. I don't want you .... (wipe) your dirty hands in the clean towel!

158. My goodness! I forgot .... (pick up) Nancy from the station!
159. I definitely remember .... (allow) him .... (use) my new bike.
160. Mother has me .... (tidy) my room.
161. My coat needs .... (clean). Don't forget .... (take) it to the dry cleaner's.
162. He stopped at the sweet shop .... (get) some cookies for his daughter.
163. He'd love .... (have) the opportunity of .... (meet) Nancy again.
164. Our teacher went on .... (explain) our homework.
165. My sewing machine needs .... (oil) every two months.
166. Having a party tonight will mean .... (clean) the whole house tomorrow.
167. Let Pit .... (study)! Leave him alone!
168. Peter likes .... (get up) early in the morning and .... (go) to bed late at night.
169. Your shoes want .... (clean).
170. It's no good .... (complain) again and again.
171. The .... (read) of books inspires your imagination.
172. I felt his hands .... (sweat).
173. Would you mind my .... (invite) you for lunch?
174. The burglar escaped .... (be) caught by the police.
175. Paul can't resist .... (drink) alcohol.
176. I need somebody tall .... (reach) the vase on the cupboard!
177. I suggest .... (call) the ambulance.
178. Mrs Miller dreads .... (be) alone in her big house.
179. Could we postpone .... (talk) to him?
180. Please pardon my .... (forget) about your birthday.
181. Grandpa's aversion to .... (iron) is awful. He can't get used to .... (help) granny with the household.
182. There is no .... (know) when he will arrive.
183. Please don't waste your time .... (hang) around and .... (do) nothing.
184. Go on .... (read), please.
185. We heard his voice .... (tremble).
186. I tried hard .... (win) the first prize, but I failed.
187. I don't fancy .... (sleep) in a tent.
188. I really hope .... (meet) him again.
189. She made him .... (cut) the hedge.

I USED TO / I AM USED TO

1. **used to + infinitive** used for a **regular habit** in the **past** and for **past** situations

   (ich tat es gewöhnlich, pflegte es zu tun)

   I **used to** play with dolls when I was a girl.
   Did you **use to** smoke when you were young?
   He **didn't use to** eat spinach when he was a boy.
   I **never used to** stay out after midnight when I was a teenager.

2. **to *be* used to + gerund**   *an etwas gewöhnt sein*
   to *get* used to + gerund   *sich an etwas gewöhnen*

   Present: She *is* **used to** getting up early in the morning.
   Sie ist es gewöhnt, früh am Morgen aufzustehen.
   She *is getting* **used to** working hard.
   Sie gewöhnt sich daran, hart zu arbeiten.
   Are you **used to** being told what you should do?
   Bist du es gewöhnt, dass man dir sagt, was du tun sollst?
   Is he *getting* **used to** living alone?
   Gewöhnt er sich daran, alleine zu leben?
   Grandfather *isn't* **used to** doing much housework.
   Großvater ist es nicht gewöhnt, viel Hausarbeit zu machen.
   I *am* **used to** having muesli in the morning.
   Ich bin es gewöhnt am Morgen Müsli zu essen.

   Past tense: He *was* **used to** taking care of his little sister.
   He *got* **used to** taking care of his little sister.
   Were you **used to** cooking when you were a teenager?
   Did he *get* **used to** Nancy's smoking?
   I *wasn't* **used to** drinking alcohol when I was young.

   Future: He **will** *be* **used** to working hard.
   Er wird daran gewöhnt sein, hart zu arbeiten.
   He **will** *get* **used to** working hard.
   Er wird sich daran gewöhnen, hart zu arbeiten.
   Will he *be* **used** to being married one day?
   Will he *get* **used to** looking after the baby?

   Pres. perf: I **have(n't)** *got* **used to** his playing the drums yet.

USED TO WITH INFINITIVE OR GERUND

1. Sandra isn't used to .... (drink) much alcohol.
2. After her holidays she found it hard to get up in the morning. She wasn't used to .... (get) up at six any more.
3. Our neighbours' party room used to .... (be) an indoor swimming pool once.
4. He is used to .... (live) as a single man. He doesn't mind it.
5. Mary won't get used to .... (be) divorced.
6. I wasn't used to .... (take) care of my sister's three little children but finally I've got used to it now.
7. He didn't use to .... (like) spinach, but now he is very fond of it.
8. When I was a child I used to .... (watch) animal cartoons, but now I find them boring.
9. Susan used to .... (wear) short hair, but now she wants to grow it.
10. Robert is used to .... (cook), ... (do) the washing and .... (iron).
11. He used to .... (be) a lazy student, but since he met Carol he has been studying hard.
12. She used to .... (go) jogging every day, but when she broke her leg she gave it up.
13. Have you met Sarah? She never used .... (be) fat, but now she has put on weight.
14. We are used to .... (go) on a camping holiday. So we don't mind sleeping on the ground.
15. She used to .... (drink) a lot of coffee, but now she's stopped it because of her high blood pressure.
16. Father used to .... (smoke) twenty cigarettes a day. But now he's stopped smoking.
17. When I was a student I was used to .... (have) little money.
18. When she was thirteen she didn't use to .... (go) to discos, but now she goes there every weekend.
19. We are going to spend our holiday in Ireland. So we must get used to .... (drive) on the left.
20. When father was a child he didn't use to .... (get) much pocket money.
21. We live in Innsbruck now, but we used to .... (live) in Linz.
22. The boutique used to .... (be) a bakery once.

GERUND SHORTENS SENTENCES

1. only one subject:

He remembered <u>that</u> **he** had met her.
He remembered having met her. *(written, formal English)*
He remembered meeting her. *(spoken English)*
(Er erinnerte sich daran, dass er sie gesehen hat/te.)

2. two subjects:

He remembered <u>that</u> **she** had greeted him.
He remembered **her** having greeted him. *(written, formal English)*
He remembered **her** greeting him. *(spoken English)*
(Er erinnerte sich daran, dass sie ihn gegrüßt hat/te.)

if	⇨	**by**	+	gerund	*dadurch dass*
and/but not	⇨	**without**	+	gerund	*ohne zu*
(al)though	⇨	**in spite of**	+	gerund	*Obwohl, trotz*
when	⇨	**on**	+	gerund	*als, sobald als*
as, because	⇨	**for/with/by**	+	gerund	*wegen, da ja, indem, weil*
		because of/ from/after			
before	⇨	**before**	+	gerund	*bevor*
after	⇨	**after**	+	gerund	*nachdem*
--------	⇨	**instead of**	+	gerund	*anstatt*

Examples:

If he jumps into the water, he will save the girl.
By jumping into the water he will save the girl.

He came in **and didn't** knock at the door.
He came in **without knocking** at the door.

Though he had passed the exam he wasn't happy.
In spite of passing the exam he wasn't happy.

When I saw her I greeted her politely.
On seeing her I greeted her politely.

We didn't get home **because** we missed the train.
We didn't get home **because of missing** the train.

We came home late after midnight **because** we had missed the train.
We came home late after midnight **because of missing** the train.

She was angry **because** she didn't find her book.
She was angry **at not finding** her book.

He got a prize **because** he won the race.
He got a prize **for winning** the race.

Her arms hurt **because** she carried two heavy bags.
Her arms hurt **from carrying** two heavy bags.

She sounded hoarse **because** she had shouted so much.
She sounded hoarse **after/because of shouting** so much.

Before he went to town he phoned his friend.
Before going to town he phoned his friend.

Do something about it! Don't complain!
Do something about it **instead of complaining**!

USE GERUND CONSTRUCTIONS

1. Don't complain! Try to work harder.
2. He is angry with me because I called him a liar.
3. He went away and didn't take his umbrella with him.
4. If you try hard you will win.
5. I don't use my computer to write personal letters.
6. She earns some money because she does silk painting.
7. I must thank you because you paid back the money in time.
8. He was able to escape the police because he jumped out of the window.
9. She suggested that we could go to the cinema.
10. After we had found a nice B&B, we went to bed.
11. When I met him I gave him my address.
12. The boy denied that he had stolen her purse.
13. I cannot understand that Simon is so angry.
14. He greeted her but he didn't look into her eyes.
15. Her eyes were red because she had been weeping.
16. Before he went to bed he closed the window.
17. Though Sam had everything he wanted he was unhappy.
18. Before I have my breakfast I usually take a shower.
19. After he had got a bad mark, he decided to study harder.
20. He is depressed because he has no job.
21. Billy ran across the road but he didn't look.
22. Lilly was afraid that the cat would scratch her.
23. Do you mind if I open the window for a moment?
24. I still remember when I fell in love for the first time.
25. If you are so loud you will wake up the baby.
26. I have got special scissors. With them you can cut metal as well as cloth.
27. After he had finished lunch, he took a nap.
28. Although Frank eats very little he is rather fat.
29. Don't hang around! You should read a good book.
30. When we arrived in Paris we phoned our friends.
31. You will get some extra pocket money if you mow Mr Spencer's lawn.
32. Before he entered the house he emptied the letter box.
33. I want to give him a little present because he was so kind to us.
34. After he had won the game, he was exhausted.
35. Sandy is unhappy that he must remain in bed.
36. He didn't go home but went to a bar.
37. He doesn't mind if we invite Robert to our party.
38. She watches TV all day. She should help in the garden.
39. I still remember when he arrived.
40. After I had eaten lots of whipped cream, I felt sick.

CONDITIONAL

Revise ☺ III pages 7–13, pages 65–68 first

1. If you go away, please .... (lock) the door carefully.
2. If I were you, I .... (leave) earlier to avoid stress.
3. Unless he runs, he .... (miss) the last train.
4. Pupils would love him if he .... (be) a bit warm-hearted.
5. If she had not left him, she .... (not / be) in trouble now.
6. You can rely on me if you .... (need) help.
7. He would have had breakfast if it .... (not / be) so late.
8. I would have met Paul if I .... (go) to Pit's party yesterday.
9. If he hadn't hurt her, she .... (not / be) angry with him now.
10. I .... (be) happy if you could inform Peter.
11. She wouldn't have survived if he .... (not / help) her.
12. If we don't phone, mum .... (be) worried.
13. If Pit took the job overseas, she .... (be) desperate.
14. If he hadn't taken me to the train, I .... (miss) it.
15. If you don't like children, you .... (mustn't) become a teacher.

CONTACT CLAUSES

Revise ☺ III pages 78–85 first.
Contact clauses are **relative clauses** where the relative pronoun can be **omitted**. This is the case when they are **objects**. *(Contact clauses sind Relativsätze, in denen das Relativpronomen ausgelassen werden kann. Dies ist der Fall, wenn sie Objekt sind.)*

Fill in relative pronouns. Put them into brackets, if they are not necessary:

1. The film .... father had forbidden us to watch was a horror film.
2. This is the man .... daughter is having twins.
3. The boy .... invited her to the cinema is Laura's son.
4. The car .... I saw Frank drive with was a Ferrari.
5. This is the woman .... Bill would love to marry.
6. The dog .... my neighbour feeds every day is Mr Miller's dog.
7. The cap .... is lying on the chair is Tom's.
8. He said that he would always love her, ... was not true.
9. .... I really hate is fishburgers.
10. Unfortunately this is all .... I can do for you.

PAST PERFECT TENSE PROGRESSIVE

For the use of past perfect simple see ☺ **III** page 60, ☺ **IV** page 10.

1. Formation: *had been + ing form*

Examples: I *had been working*
she *had been running*
we *had been waiting*

2. Use:

We use the *past perfect tense progressive* to say <u>how long</u> something *had been happening* <u>before</u> something else happened / was done. <u>Duration</u> **is stressed.**
(*Wir verwenden die past perfect progressive tense, um zu sagen, wie lange etwas bereits geschehen war, <u>bevor</u> etwas anderes geschah/gemacht wurde. Dauer ist betont.*)

Study the following examples:

We **had not been waiting** very long before he arrived.
They **had been working** all day, that's why they were so tired.
It **had been snowing** for two hours before we decided to go out.
He **had been lying** in bed for two weeks before he died.
After she **had been having** an unhappy love affair, she went to America.
Sue **had been watching** TV for a long time, that's why her eyes were red.
The boys **had been playing** for only five minutes when she called them in.
After she **had been having** a nightmare, she was wet with sweat.
They **had been having** a barbecue when suddenly a storm came up.
She**'d been dancing** all night long, that's why her feet hurt.
We**'d been laughing** a lot until the teacher came in.
She **had been crying** before she left.

> **Attention:** For the list of verbs that are normally **not used in progressive form** see ☺ **III** page 27.

PARTICIPLE

The PARTICIPLE is an **ing-form** and can be used in the **active** and the **passive** form.

	active	passive
Present	seeing	being seen
Perfect	having seen	having been seen

1. It is used as an **adjective**.

Examples: the **running** boy
the **sleeping** baby
an **exciting** book

2. It is used with the **progressive** (= continuous) forms

Examples: I am **working** now.
You were **sleeping** from one to three.
We have been **having** a wonderful time.
After they had been **shopping**, they were tired.
At this time tomorrow we will be **flying** to Paris.

3. It is used after following verbs:

see*	look at*	go
hear*	listen to*	come
watch*	feel*	sit
notice*	smell	stand
observe* (beobachten)	find	remain (bleiben)

* also see: OBJECT WITH THE INFINITIVE WITHOUT TO page 47

Examples:
I *saw* her **coming**.
We *heard* her **crying**.
She *watched* him **running** away.
They *observed* us **swimming** in the lake.
He *noticed* me **buying** cigarettes.

Spot the difference:

Participle:

I *saw* him **climbing** the tree.   ⇨   **action** is important   *(Handlung)*
I saw him while he was climbing the tree.

Infinitive without to:

I *saw* him **climb** the tree.   ⇨   **fact** is important   *(Tatsache)*
I saw that he climbed the tree.

Examples:
She *looked at* him **dancing** with Sue.
Let's *listen to* Tom **playing** the recorder.
I *felt* her **trembling**.
I *smell* something **burning** in the kitchen.
I *found* him **lying** on the floor.
We *went* **shopping**.
Tom *came* **running**.
He was *sitting* on the sofa **reading** a book.
We *stood* **watching** them.
He *remained* **sitting**.

4. It is used instead of adverbial and relative clauses and conjunctions:

Examples:
When they saw me they ran away. *(adverbial clause)*
Seeing me they ran away. *(participle construction)*
(On seeing me they ran away.) *(gerund construction)*
also revise GERUND SHORTENS SENTENCES pages 86–88

After we had slept well, we felt fresh again. *(adverbial clause)*
Having slept well we felt fresh again. *(participle construction)*
(After sleeping well we felt fresh again.) *(gerund construction)*
*Remember: with **after** we prefer **sleeping** to having slept: Key p 113 (page 88) sentences 10, 19, 27, 34, 40.*

I saw the man **as** he was waiting for his friend. *(adverbial clause)*
I saw the man **waiting** for his friend. *(participle construction)*

The woman **who/that** is buying the pink hat is Mrs Schneider. *(relative clause)*
The woman **buying** the pink hat is Mrs Schneider. *(participle construction)*

The ring **which/that** is lying on the table is mother's. *(relative clause)*
The ring **lying** on the table is mother's. *(participle construction)*

As he was ill he went to bed. *(conjunction)*
Being ill he went to bed. *(participle construction)*
(He went to bed for being ill. He went to bed because of being ill.) *(gerund construction)*

The burglars rushed in **and** shouted, "Hands up!" *(conjunction)*
The burglars rushed in **shouting**, "Hands up!" *(participle construction)*

The boy ran away **and** wept loudly. *(conjunction)*
The boy ran away **weeping** loudly. *(participle construction)*

Attention: Mind the word order!

Eating a mouse we were watching a cat.	⇨	nonsense *(Unsinn)*
We were watching a cat eating a mouse.	⇨	correct
Building a nest we saw a bird.	⇨	nonsense *(Unsinn)*
We saw a bird building a nest.	⇨	correct

USE PARTICIPLE CONSTRUCTIONS

1. The old man was sitting on a bench and was sleeping.
2. After he had taken a seat, he ordered a pint of beer.
3. After they had eaten, they cleared the table.
4. As I felt rather exhausted, I lay down a bit.
5. She was lying on the floor and was writing her diary.
6. Is there anybody that wishes to talk to me?
7. Mrs Brown was on her way home. She was talking to herself.
8. I was reading a book in bed. I fell asleep.
9. After she had written the letter, she took it to the post office.
10. As she didn't know his phone number, she couldn't call him.
11. We saw some people who were swimming in the cold river.
12. When I arrrived I noticed a policeman who was standing behind my car.
13. After we had bought some food, we began to cook.
14. She entered the room and smiled at everybody.
15. When he ran after the bus, he lost his key.
16. I watched the little girl as she was picking flowers.
17. While mum was preparing dinner she cut herself.
18. As Peter had drunk too much wine, he felt sick.
19. The boys who were waiting in front of the school are Sally's friends.
20. I saw Bob how he kissed Barbara.
21. After Bill had come in, he took off his shoes.
22. He fell down and hit his head on the floor.
23. She knew that she might lose so she gave up.
24. When Tom jumped into the pond, he lost his bathing trunks.
25. As Simon was a good swimmer, he won the competition
26. We felt that the house was shaking.
27. He came in and greeted us politely.
28. After Mr Spencer had done all the ironing, he lit his pipe.
29. He feared that the police might find his gun, so he hid it in the shed.
30. As she didn't know how to interpret the poem, she was silent.
31. When she drank from her mug, she burnt her lips.
32. As time rushed along, we had to run in order to catch our train.
33. As the weather was very nice, we decided to go on a trip.
34. After he had read the brochures, he chose to go to Ireland that summer.
35. When we approached the house, we saw that a window had been broken.
36. Sue asked her father and hoped he would know the answer.
37. As she hadn't eaten a good breakfast, she was hungry.
38. He rushed out of the room and slammed the door.
39. The train that is standing on platform four goes to Vienna.
40. The woman got out of the bus. She carried two heavy bags.
41. He thought about the answer and bit his lips.

WORDS

accept	akzeptieren, annehmen	cleanup	Reinigungsaktion
admire	bewundern	clear away	wegräumen
advice	Rat	come round	vorbeikommen
advise	raten	compare	vergleichen
afford	sich leisten können	competition	Wettkampf
afterwards	nachher	complain	sich beklagen
allergic to	allergisch	complaint	Beschwerde
ambulance	Rettung	composition	Aufsatz
annoyed	verärgert	compromise	Kompromiss
applaud	applaudieren	concentrate on	sich konzentrieren auf
approach	sich nähern	consider	betrachten, halten für
appropriate	passend, geeignet	constant	dauernd
argue	streiten	cough	husten
assassinate	ermorden	customs officer	Zöllner
at once	sofort	customs	Zoll
attempt	versuchen	damage	kaputt machen
attention	Aufmerksamkeit	date	ausgehen mit
attract	auf sich richten, erregen	defend	verteidigen
avoid	vermeiden	definitely	bestimmt, genau
B&B	Zimmer mit Frühstück	delightful	bezaubernd, reizend
bakery	Bäckerei	deserve	verdienen
bar of chocolate	Tafel Schokolade	desire	wünschen, ersehnen
bathing trunks	Badehose	desperate	verzweifelt
be fed up with	es satthaben	developing	Entwicklungs-
be grounded	Hausarrest haben	diary	Tagebuch
beggar	Bettler	disappointed	enttäuscht
behave	sich benehmen	disease	Krankheit
behaviour	Benehmen	dismay	Entsetzen
beneath	unterhalb	dismiss	entlassen
bike (to)	Fahrrad fahren	disturb	stören
bill	Rechnung	divorced	geschieden
bored	gelangweilt	dough	Teig
bother	sich die Mühe machen	drug	Droge
brackets	Klammern	dull	langweilig
brand-new	nagelneu	dustbin	Mülleimer
bring along	mitbringen	dye	färben
brochure	Broschüre	election	Wahl
bunch	Strauß	else	noch
calculation	Rechnung	empty (to)	ausleeren
campaign	Kampagne	engaged	besetzt; verlobt
camping site	Campingplatz	enormous	enorm
candle	Kerze	entertainment	Unterhaltung
can't stand	nicht ertagen können	environment	Umwelt
cardboard	Karton	exhausted	erschöpft
ceiling	Zimmerdecke	experience (to)	erleben
cellar	Keller	experience	Erfahrung
cereals	Getreideprodukte	fault	Fehler
charming	charmant, bezaubernd	fence	Gartenzaun
chat	Unterhaltung	final	endgültig
circumstance	Umstand	fire	feuern
city authority	Stadtverwaltung	flee	flüchten

foolish	*dumm*	last (to)	*dauern*
force	*zwingen*	lawn	*Rasen*
forgive	*verzeihen*	lawyer	*Rechtsanwalt*
form	*Formular*	left-hander	*Linkshänder*
free-range eggs	*Eier von freilaufenden Hühnern*	legibly (Adv.)	*leserlich*
		liar	*Lügner*
freeze	*frieren*	library	*Bücherei*
fridge	*Kühlschrank*	lie	*Lüge, lügen*
frustrated	*frustriert*	lifestyle	*Lebensstil*
fuel	*Benzin*	light – lit	*anzünden – zündete an*
get away with	*davonkommen mit*	local paper	*Lokalzeitung*
get to know	*kennenlernen*	long for	*sich sehnen*
go jogging	*joggen*	looker	*gutaussehende Person*
go steady with	*fix gehen mit*	madness	*Verrücktheit*
greenhouse	*Glashaus*	mag	*Magazin, Zeitung*
guest	*Gast*	make fun of	*auslachen*
hand in	*abgeben*	manage	*schaffen*
handle	*umgehen mit*	maniac	*Verrückte(r)*
handsome	*fesch*	marvellous	*wunderbar*
handwriting	*Handschrift*	mention	*erwähnen*
hang about	*herumhängen*	message	*Botschaft*
haunted	*verwunschen*	milk carton	*Milchpackerl*
have a crush on	*auf jem. „stehen"*	motorway	*Autobahn*
headmaster	*Schuldirektor*	mow	*mähen*
headquarters	*Hauptquartier*	mug	*Becher, Häferl*
health care	*Gesundheitsfürsorge*	mustard	*Senf*
heart attack	*Herzinfarkt*	nag	*nörgeln*
hedge	*Hecke*	nap	*Nickerchen*
hike, hiking	*wandern*	nibble	*knabbern*
hoarse	*heiser*	nonsense	*Unsinn*
housing estate	*Wohnanlage*	notice	*bemerken*
hoover	*staubsaugen*	observe	*beobachten, bemerken*
hug	*umarmen*	obvious	*offensichtlich*
hurt	*verletzen*	passenger	*Fahrgast*
illness	*Krankheit*	permit	*erlauben*
imagination	*Vorstellungskraft*	persuade	*überreden*
impressed	*beeindruckt*	pint of beer	*Glas Bier*
in advance	*im Voraus*	pity	*bemitleiden*
include	*dazugeben, beilegen*	pleased	*erfreut*
inhabitants	*Bewohner*	pray	*beten*
insist on	*darauf bestehen*	pretty	*ziemlich; hübsch*
inspire	*inspirieren*	prison	*Gefängnis*
instruction	*Anleitung*	promise	*versprechen*
interrupt	*unterbrechen*	properly	*ordentlich*
introduce	*einführen; jemanden vorstellen*	published	*veröffentlicht*
		punishment	*Bestrafung*
invent	*erfinden*	purse	*Geldtasche*
invention	*Erfindung*	rather	*ziemlich*
invitation	*Einladung*	recipe	*Rezept*
keen on	*erpicht auf*	refreshing	*erfrischend*
keep in mind	*beachten, sich merken*	refugee	*Flüchtling*
knit	*stricken*	refuse	*sich weigern, ablehnen*
knock over	*umschütten*		

relaxing	*entspannend*	twins	*Zwillinge*
remember	*sich selbst erinnern*	typewriter	*Schreibmaschine*
remind	*jem. erinnern*	tyre	*Reifen*
reservation	*Reservat*	unexpected	*unerwartet*
Retsina	*geharzter griech. Wein*	unfortunately	*unglücklicherweise*
ripe	*reif*	unpleasant	*unangenehm*
rock face	*Felswand*	view	*Aussicht*
rough	*rauh*	violence	*Gewalt*
rush	*sausen*	voice	*Stimme*
scissors (pl.)	*Schere*	war	*Krieg*
scratch	*kratzen*	warm-hearted	*herzlich*
scuba diving	*Sporttauchen*	wasp	*Wespe*
severe	*schwer, streng*	weight	*Gewicht*
shed	*Schuppen, Häuschen*	where else	*wo sonst noch*
sign	*Tafel, Zeichen*	whipped cream	*Schlagobers*
singing pub	*Pub mit Musik*	whisper	*flüstern*
single mother	*alleinerziehende Mutter*	whistle	*pfeifen*
slam	*zuschlagen*	worry	*sich Sorgen machen*
slurp	*schlürfen*	wrap up	*einpacken*
soap opera	*Seifenoper*		
soldier	*Soldat*		
sore throat	*rauer Hals, Halsweh*		
speech	*Rede*		
starvation	*Verhungern*		
steep	*steil*		
stepsister	*Stiefschwester*		
stir	*rühren*		
stranger	*Fremder*		
straw	*Strohhalm*		
strength	*Kraft, Stärke*		
stretch	*strecken*		
suck	*saugen*		
suffer from	*leiden an*		
suggestion	*Vorschlag*		
suitable	*passend*		
survive	*überleben*		
sweat	*schwitzen*		
take a joke	*Spaß verstehen*		
tar	*teeren*		
tear	*Träne*		
thirst	*Durst*		
thunderstorm	*Gewitter*		
tin	*Dose*		
tiptoe	*auf Zehenspitzen gehen*		
trashy	*schundig*		
treat	*behandeln*		
treatment	*Behandlung*		
tremble	*zittern*		
tribe	*Stamm*		
trust	*vertrauen*		

KEY

page 1

1. faster (☺ II p33/1a), fast, more comfortable (☺ II p35/2c), nicer (☺ II p33/1a), more expensive (☺ II p35/2c)
2. most exciting (☺ II p35/2c)
3. marvellous
4. rougher, hotter and drier (☺ II p33/1a)
5. most marvellous (☺ II p35/2c)
6. more fascinating (☺ II p35/2c)
7. better, better (☺ II p35/3)
8. best (☺ II p35/3)
9. worst (☺ II p35/3)
10. severer (☺ II p34/1c)
11. unpleasant, best (☺ II p35/3), handsomest (☺ II p34/1c), cleverest (☺ II p33/1b)
12. latest (☺ II p37), brand-new
13. stronger, stronger (☺ II p33/1a)
14. most spectacular (☺ II p35/2c)
15. greatest (☺ II p33/1a), more relaxing (☺ II p35/2c)
16. more dangerous (☺ II p35/2c)
17. nearest (☺ II p37)
18. fewer (☺ II p33/1a), healthy
19. most interesting (☺ II p35/2c)
20. next (☺ II p37), big / bigger (☺ II p33/1a)
21. fewer (☺ II p33/1a), last (☺ II p37), beautiful
22. more difficult / less difficult (☺ II p35/2c), last (☺ II p37)

page 2

1. somebody / someone (☺ II p18/1)
2. something / somebody / someone (☺ II p18/1)
3. anybody / anyone (☺ II p19/1)
4. anything (☺ II p19/1)
5. any (☺ II p19/1), some (☺ II p18/1)
6. something, some, some (☺ II p18/2)
7. somehow (☺ II p18/1)
8. any (☺ II p19/1), some (☺ II p18/1)
9. any (☺ II p19/1)
10. any (☺ II p19/2) / some (☺ II p18/2)
11. somewhere (☺ II p18/1)
12. some (☺ II p18/1)
13. some (☺ II p18/1)
14. somewhere (☺ II p18/1)
15. any (☺ II p19/2), any (☺ II p19/1)
16. any (☺ II p19/1)
17. any (☺ II p19/1)
18. somewhere (☺ II p18/2), anywhere (☺ II p19/2), somewhere (☺ II p18/1)
19. any (☺ II p19/4)
20. some, somewhere (☺ II p18/1), anything (☺ II p19/1)
21. some (☺ II p18/1)
22. some (☺ II p18/1)
23. any (☺ II p19/4)
24. somebody / someone (☺ II p18/1)
25. somewhere (☺ II p18/1)
26. some (☺ II p18/2), any (☺ II p19/1)
27. somebody / someone (☺ II p18/1)
28. something (☺ II p18/1)
29. somehow (☺ II p18/1)
30. anybody / anyone (☺ II p19/3)
31. anybody / anyone (☺ II p19/1)

page 3

1. was stolen, was arrested
2. will be repaired
3. is going to be painted / will be painted
4. were washed
5. is needed / will be needed
6. will be dismissed
7. has not been beaten
8. were driven away, were killed, were placed
9. is seen / was seen
10. is named, were built
11. are made / were made
12. is made
13. is called
14. was assassinated
15. was baked
16. had been shot in
17. was being repaired
18. is being tarred, cannot be used
19. was sold / had been sold
20. must be done
21. may be invited
22. ought to be given
23. was produced

page 4

1. good (☺ III p 39)
2. extremely (☺ III p 34c) slowly (☺ III p 38)
3. pretty (☺ III p 37) badly (☺ III p 34c)
4. friendly *(Adjective after is – Hilfsverb)*
5. short (☺ III p 37)
6. deeply (☺ III p 37)
7. extremely small (☺ III p 34b)
8. fast (☺ III p 36)
9. horrible (☺ III p 39)
10. readily (☺ III p 37)
11. really (wie: ☺ III p 35) highly (☺ III p 37), badly (☺ III p 34a)
12. closely (☺ III p 37)
13. nervously (☺ III p 39, *Exceptions*)
14. angry (☺ III p 39)
15. pretty (☺ III p 39), prettily (☺ III p 37)
16. dark (☺ III p 39)
17. direct (☺ III p 37)
18. quickly (☺ III p 34a)
19. awfully (☺ III p 34b) bitter (☺ III p 39)
20. monthly (☺ III p 35)
21. easily (☺ III p 35, ☺ III p 34a)
22. highly (☺ III p 37) dangerous (☺ III p 34b)
23. right(ly) (☺ III p 38)
24. carefully (☺ III p 39, *Exceptions*)
25. dearly (☺ III p 37)
26. soft (☺ III p 39)
27. in a lively way/manner/fashion (☺ III p 36)
28. carefully (☺ III p 39, *Exceptions*)
29. lately (☺ III p 36)
30. false (☺ III p 37)
31. severely (☺ III p 34b)

page 8

1. up
2. down
3. away / off
4. up
5. out
6. off
7. through / out
8. up
9. up
10. about
11. along
12. on to
13. on
14. on
15. on
16. into
17. up (Dinge beschleunigen)
18. away with
19. up
20. off/out
21. up with
22. to
23. out
24. off
25. on to
26. on
27. up with
28. up
29. through
30. for
31. into
32. up
33. on
34. up
35. up
36. down
37. away / off
38. off
39. in
40. on, at

page 9

1. should have done
2. should have helped
3. ought to have phoned
4. should have prepared
5. should have visited
6. ought to have paid
7. could have been
8. could have taken, mightn't have seen
9. may have been
10. may have been
11. may have found, might have danced
12. ought to have given
13. oughtn't to have told
14. may have been jealous
15. oughtn't to have kissed

page 10

1. will be (☺ II p 45 A)
2. will work (☺ II p 45 A)
3. are going to collect (☺ II p 47 A,C)
4. is going to plant (☺ II p 47 A,C)
5. will destroy (☺ II p 45 D)
6. is going to win (☺ II p 47 B)
7. won't be (☺ II p 45 A,D)
8. are going to organize (☺ II p 47 A,C)
9. will possibly start (☺ II p 45 A)
10. will ('ll) order (☺ II p 45 C)
11. are going to buy (☺ II p 47 A,C)
12. will go (☺ II p 45 A)
13. am going to explain (☺ II p 47 A,C)
14. will ('ll) explain (☺ II p 45 C)
15. is going to marry (☺ II p 47 B)

*

1. had already left
2. had eaten
3. had just managed
4. had taken
5. had lost
6. had run
7. had forgotten
8. had given
9. had hoovered

pages 14, 15

1. She asked me if I had recognized him by his voice. (☺ IV p 12/2, ☺ III p 69/2) (*Anmerkung: Wenn ein Personalobjekt hinter dem Frageverb steht, z.B. me, her, him, us, you, them, kann man nur **ask** nicht aber inquire, enquire, wonder, want to know verwenden.*)
2. He asked / inquired / wanted to know / **if** I / we could get hold of a ... for him. (☺ IV p 12 /2, ☺ III p 70/3) *(Hier sind alle Frageverben einsetzbar, weil kein Personalobjekt folgt!)*
3. Bob wanted to know **why** I / we hadn't shown ... (☺ IV p 12 /1, ☺ III p 69/2)
4. I wondered **if** she / he ... had included .... (☺ IV p 12 /2, ☺ III p 69/2)
5. He asked / inquired / wanted to know / **where** he would find *(würde)* / **where** he should find *(finden sollte)* his group ... (☺ IV p 12 /1, p 13/3)
6. He asked me / him / her ... **where** I / he / she ... had spent my / his / her last ... (☺ IV p 12/1, ☺ III p 69/2)
7. Billy asked me **/** was curious to know **/ how long** Sally had been going ... (☺ IV p 12/1, ☺ III p 69/2)
8. ... **if** he had been frustrated when I had told him ... (☺ IV p 12/2, ☺ III p 69/2)
9. ... **if** I would look after the children *(ob ich würde)* (*Anmerkung: if heißt ob und kann daher auch mit would stehen! Vergleiche: if = wenn, falls* ☺ III p 9 ff). / Mum asked me to look after ... *(bat mich)* (☺ IV p12/2, p 13/4, ☺ III p 69/2)
10. He asked / inquired / enquired / wanted to know / **when** we were going to meet ... (☺ IV p12/1, ☺ III p 69/2)
11. Robert asked / inquired / enquired / wanted to know / **how** she always got away ... (☺ IV p12/1, ☺ III p 69/2)

12. ... **if** she should come round <u>the following day</u>./ ... **if** she was to come round ... *(sollen)* (☺ IV p 13/3)
13. ... **why** he was / she was / you were ... (☺ IV p 12/1, ☺ III p 69/2)
14. ... **if** the noise had kept me / us awake. (☺ IV p 12/2, ☺ III p 69/2)
15. ... **how often** <u>the girl</u> / <u>her girl-friend</u> had mentioned ... (☺ IV p12/1, ☺ III p 69/2, p73/ *Attention*/2)
16. He asked / inquired / wanted to know / **if** I / we would meet her ... *(Anmerkung: if heißt ob und kann daher auch mit would stehen! Vergleiche: if = wenn, falls* ☺ III p 9 ff) (☺ IV p12/2, p 13/4, ☺ III p 69/2)
17. ... **if** we should invite her ... *(sollen)* / **if** we would invite her ... *(würden)* (☺ IV p 12/2, p 13/3)
18. ... **how often** I had dated... (☺ IV p 12/1, ☺ III p 69/2)
19. ... **why** they were always making fun of <u>his friend</u> / <u>the man</u> ... (☺ IV p12/1, ☺ III p 69/2, p73/ *Attention*/2)
20. Mary asked / inquired / wanted to know / **if** he really hadn't taken ... (☺ IV p 12/2, ☺ III p 69/2)
21. ... **if** we / they should send him ... / **if** he / they were to send ... *(sollen)* (☺ IV p 12/2, p 13/3)
22. ... **why** I / we couldn't / **why** I wasn't / we weren't able to concentrate on my / our ...
    (☺ IV p12/1, ☺ III p69/2)
23. She asked me **if** I had known that Julian had a crush on Linda. (☺ IV p 12/2, ☺ III p 69/2)
24. He asked / inquired / wanted to know / **for how long** they would be able to stay ... (☺ IV p 12/1, ☺ II p 6)
25. ... **where** I / we usually bought my / our meat. (☺ IV p 12/1, ☺ III p 69/2)
26. ... **where** she would be <u>that</u> time <u>the following year</u>. *(sein würde)* (☺ IV p 12/1, p 13/3)
27. ... **whose** cap it was. (☺ IV p 12/1, ☺ III p 69/2)
28. ... want**s** to know *(Attention! No change of tenses after verb in present!)* **if** I am / we are thirsty **and if**
    I would/ we would like ... (☺ IV p 12/2, ☺ III p 69/1)
29. ... **who** had cleared ... (☺ IV p 12/1, ☺ III p 69/2)
30. He asked / inquired / wanted to know / **when** we / they would be back ... *(würden)* / should be back / were to be back *(sollten)*... (☺ IV p 12/1, p 13/3)
31. ... asked / was interested in **how long** the trip would last. (☺ IV p 12/1, p 13/4, ☺ III p 69/2)
32. Fred asked / inquired / enquired / wanted to know / **if** I was / we were sure that they wanted to introduce ...
    (☺ IV p 12/2, ☺ III p 69/2)
33. The teacher asked / inquired / enquired / wanted to know / was interested in / **how much** time it had taken
    me / us to do my /our work. (☺ IV p 12/1, ☺ III p 69/2)
34. He asked / inquired / enquired / wanted to know / **if** it was true that Bill was not ... (☺ IV p 12/2, ☺ III p 69/2)
35. Ben asked / wanted to know **if** I <u>would like</u> (to have) a drink with him. / Ben offered me a drink. / Ben invited me to have a drink (with him). / Ben invited me for a drink. (☺ IV p 12/2, p 13/4)
36. ... **from where** they had had to flee. (☺ IV p 12/1, ☺ III p 69/2, ☺ III p 64 *modal verbs in past perfect*)
37. ... **if** I would like a sandwich <u>then</u>. (☺ IV p 12/2, ☺ III p 70/3)
38. He asked / inquired / enquired / wanted to know / **if** <u>the man</u> had really refused to help ...
    (☺ IV p 12/2, ☺ III p 69/2, p 73 *Attention*/2)
39. She ask**s** *(Present!)* me **where** she shall find ... *(finden soll)* (☺ IV p 12/1, p 13/3, ☺ III p 69/1)
40. Phil asked / inquired / enquired / wanted to know / **if** I / we had already read ... (☺ IV p 12 /2, ☺ III p 69/2)
41. He asked / inquired / enquired / wanted to know / **if** your / our school mag had been ... (☺IV p12/2,☺III p69/2)
42. ... **why** she had walked off ... (☺ IV p 12/1, ☺ III p 69/2)
43. ... **if** I thought (that) Pam would hug him. (☺ IV p 12/2, ☺ III p 69/2)
44. He asked / inquired / enquired / wanted to know / **if** my / our teacher could take ... (☺ IV p 12/2, ☺ III p 69/2)
45. ... **if** I had seen him smile. (☺ IV p 12/2, ☺ III p 69/2) *(Achtung: <u>smile</u> ist <u>Infinitiv ohne to</u> nach see*
    (☺ IV p 47) *und deshalb unveränderlich wie alle Infinitive!)*
46. ... **who** had been late for school. (☺ IV p 12/1, ☺ III p 69/2)
47. Betty asked / inquired / enquired / wanted to know / **if** they had really kissed ... (☺ IV p 12/2, ☺ III p 69/2)
48. ... **if** he might give me ... (☺ IV p 12/2, ☺ III p 69/2)
49. He asked / inquired / enquired / wanted to know / **how long** it would take me / you / us / them to clean
    my / your / their / room.(☺ IV p 12/2, ☺ III p 69/2)
50. ... **which** dress she should buy. (☺ IV p 12/1, ☺ III p 70/3)
51. ... **if** he admired Tom Hanks. (☺ IV p 12/2, ☺ III p 69/2)
52. Mandy asked / inquired / enquired / wanted to know / **how much** I had paid for <u>that</u> ...(☺IV p12/1, ☺III p69/2)
53. ... **how much** I had had to pay for it. (☺ IV p 12/1, ☺ III p 69/2, ☺ III p 64 *modal verbs*)
54. ... **why** Simon should be grounded *(Hausarrest haben sollte)* (☺ IV p 12/1, p 13/3)
55. He asked / inquired / enquired / wanted to know / **if** I / we thought she would love ... (☺IV p12/2,☺III p69/2)
56. ... **whose** house that was, just opposite ... (☺ IV p 12/1, ☺ III p 69/2)
57. ... **who** was whistling **and if** it was Tom. (☺ IV p 12/1,2, ☺ III p 69/2)
58. ... **if** it had been a ... (☺ IV p 12/2, ☺ III p 69/2)
59. ... **if** she had found ... (☺ IV p 12/2, ☺ III p 69/2)
60. ... **if** <u>her friend</u> / <u>her neighbour</u> ... / had got twins. (☺ IV p 12/2, ☺ III p 69/2, p 73 *Attention*/2)
61. ... asked / wanted to know ... **if** Phil wasn't a real looker. (☺ IV p 12/2, ☺ III p 69/2)
62. ... **if** I / we had managed to fill in ... (☺ IV p 12/2, ☺ III p 69/2)
63. He asked / inquired / enquired / wanted to know / **whose** girl-friend I / we had seen ... (☺IV p12/1, ☺IIIp 69/2)
64. ... **if** I / we had ever met ... (☺ IV p 12/2, ☺ III p 69/2)
65. ... **which** tribe lives on ... *(Attention! No change of tenses after verb in present!)* (☺ IV p 12/1, ☺ III p 69/1)
66. He asked / inquired / enquired / wanted to know / **where** the P.F. had come from. (☺ IV p 12/1, ☺ III p 69/2)
67. ... **how long** we would be away. *(würden)* / ... **how long** we should be away *(sollten)* (☺ IV p 12/1, p 13/3)
68. ... **if** the bus would be on time.*(Anmerkung: if heißt ob und kann daher auch mit would stehen!
    Vergleiche: if = wenn, falls* ☺ III p 9 ff) (☺ IV p 12/2, p 13/4, ☺ III p 69/2)

69. ... **if** I would like to have ... / She offered me a glass... / She invited me to have ... (☺ IV p 12/2, p 13/4)
70. Father asked / inquired / enquired / wanted to know / was interested in / was curious to know / **what** she had wanted to ask me / us. (☺ IV p 12/1, ☺ III p 69/2)
71. ... **if** he had really let her down. (☺ IV p 12/2, ☺ III p 69/2)
72. He asked / inquired / enquired / wanted to know / **whose** car had broken down ... the day before. (☺ IV p 12/1, ☺ III p 69/2)
73. Peter asked / inquired / enquired / wanted to know / **if** he should help me / us the following day. *(sollen)* (☺ IV p 12/1, p 13/3)
74. ... **where** else he should look for his key. *(sollen)* (☺ IV p 12/1, p 13/3)
75. He asked / inquired / enquired / wanted to know / was interested in / was curious to know / **what** kind of girl she was. (☺ IV p 12/1, ☺ III p 69/2)
76. ... **when** I would be back again. (☺ IV p 12/1, p 13/4, ☺ III p 69/2)
77. ... **when** we / they should meet in front of ... *(sollen)* / **when** we / they would meet ...*(würden)* (☺ IV p 12/1, p 13/3)
78. ... **whose** car that blue one over there was. (☺ IV p 12/1, ☺ III p 69/2)
79. ... **how long** I was / we were able to stay ... (☺ IV p 12/1, ☺ III p 69/2)
80. He asked / inquired / enquired / wanted to know / **what** had happened to Bill. (☺ IV p 12/1, ☺ III p 69/2)
81. ... **why** he refused to stay ... *(Attention! No change of tenses after verb in present!)* (☺ IV p 12/1, ☺ III p 69/1)
82. ... **how long** mum's *(Mum ist nur in der Anrede groß geschrieben)* chat would last. (☺ IV p 12/1, ☺ III p 69/2)
83. I asked *(bat)* **if** he / she ... / would introduce me to Mr. Smith. / ... **if** he / she ... / would be so kind as to introduce me to Mr Smith. / I asked him / her ... / to introduce me to Mr Smith. *(Anmerkung: **if** heißt **ob** und kann daher auch mit **would** stehen! Vergleiche: **if = wenn, falls** ☺ III p 9 ff)* (☺ IV p12/2, p13/4, ☺ III p69/2)

pages 18, 19

There are various solutions.
Here are only some suggestions.

1. He screamed / shouted at us / at me / at them / to stop that nonsense at once. / He urged us ... / commanded us ... to stop ... . / He told us .... strictly to stop ... ./ He told us ... very loudly that we ... should stop ... . (p 17/3)
2. He advised / recommended us not to talk to that man. / He suggested not talking to ... . / He suggested that we should not talk to ... *Anmerkung: suggest kann nur mit that-Konstruktion oder dem Gerund stehen.* / He warned us not to talk to ... . (p 16/2, p 17/4)
3. She told / reminded / advised / wanted me / us to have a look at my / our ... and (to) correct them. / She said that I / we should have a look at my / our ... / She said that I was / we were to have a look ... . (p 16/2)
4. She asked / begged me to take that letter to the post office for her. / She asked me if I was so kind as to take that letter to ... / She said that I should take that letter ... / She said that I should be so kind as to take ... .(p 16/1)
5. He suggested going for a walk ... / He suggested that we should go ... . (p 16/2)
   Anmerkung: suggest kann nur mit that-Konstruktion oder dem Gerund stehen.
6. The man told / advised / wanted me / us to keep away from that ... /The man said to me / us that I / we should keep away ... . (p 16/2)
7. Lucy told / begged me / us not to call him ... . (p 17/4)
8. He suggested keeping it ... / He suggested that we should keep it ... *Anmerkung: suggest kann nur mit that-Konstruktion oder dem Gerund stehen.* ... but we refused. (p 16/2, p 17/4)
9. Mum told / reminded / advised / recommended Ben to take his raincoat with him. / Mum said that Ben should take ... (p 16/2)
10. Sheila suggested taking the nine o'clock bus. / Sheila suggested that they should take the ... / Sheila recommended to take ...
    Anmerkung: suggest kann nur mit that-Konstruktion oder dem Gerund stehen. (p 16/2)
11. The teacher told / wanted us to sit down then. /The teacher said to us that we should sit down then. (p 16/2)
12. She asked / begged us to open the window. / She said to us that we should open ... / She told us to be so kind as to open the window. (p 16/1)
13. Mother asked me to help her with the cooking. / Mother said to me that I should help her with ... (p 16/1)
14. Frank warned / reminded us not to be late the following day. (p 17/4)
15. Mum came in and told us / wanted us to shut the windows because it was so cold. (p 16/2)
16. Luke asked his dad for some money. / Luke asked / begged his dad to give him some money. (p 16/1)
17. Bill told / commanded / urged his brother to leave him alone because he didn't want to be disturbed. (p 17/3)
18. I told Mary to go to Mrs Fisher and (to) bring her ... (p 16/2)
19. Father said to Tom that he wasn't allowed to watch TV then. / Father didn't allow Tom to watch TV then. / Father told Tom not to watch TV then. (p 16/2, 17/4)
20. The policeman told / ordered / wanted / commanded me to show him my ... (p 16/2, 17/3)
21. Mum asked me to get ... (p 16/1)
22. The teacher told / advised / recommended / warned him not to argue with his parents. (p 16/2, p 17/4)
23. Sally asked / begged / reminded me to write to her as soon as I was in Paris. (p 16/1/2)
24. The burglar urged / commanded / shouted at / us to put our hands in the air. (p 17/3)

25. Mandy told / ordered / commanded us to hurry up then. (p 17/3)
26. The teacher told me / us not to speak until I was / we were asked to. (p 16/2, p 17/4)
27. Mum advised / begged / asked / implored / told / dad not to drive so fast. (p 16/1/2, p 17/4)
28. Mum screamed / shouted at us / at me / at them / to stop that noise at once. /
    Mum urged me / us / commanded me / us to stop ... . / Mum told me / us strictly to stop ... . /
    Mum told me / us very loudly that I / we should stop ... . (p 17/3)
29. She reminded / told / advised / asked me not to forget to answer ... . (p 16/1/2, p 17/4)
30. Mum always tells Tom to be careful and not to run across the street. (p 16/2, p 17/4)
31. Dad asked Bill to get him some scissors.
    Dad asked Bill if he could get him ... / ... if he would be so kind as to get him some scissors. (p 16/1)
32. Mr Smith reminded / told me not to forget to call ... (p 17/4)
33. Mum told Rita to watch the cake and not to let it burn. (p 16/2, p 17/4)
34. My sister asked mum to prepare dinner then. / ... said to mum that she should prepare ... (p 16/1/2)
35. Our teacher told / wanted us to write ... (p 16/2)
36. Mum suggested that Phil should take off his coat because it was too warm in there. /
    Mum advised / recommended Phil to take off ... (p 16/2)
37. The policeman ordered / told the man to get out of his car and to be quick. (p 16/2, p 17/3)
38. The customs officer told / ordered / commanded me / us to open my / our suitcase. (p 16/2, p 17/3)
39. The detective told the driver to follow that taxi quickly. /
    The detective told the driver that he should follow that taxi quickly. (p 16/2)
40. Mrs Swan told / ordered / asked her son not to jump like mad. /
    Mrs Swan said to her son that he shouldn't jump like mad. (p 16/2, p 17/4)
41. He begged / asked me to wait for him ... (p 16/1)
42. Sue told / reminded her mum not to forget to feed the mice and (to) give them water. (p 17/4) /
    Sue said to her mum that she should not forget to ... (p 16/2)
43. Mum told / advised / recommended Nick not to eat too many sweets because it was bad for his teeth.
    (p 16/2, p 17/4)
44. Father asked mum to buy ... / Father said to mum that she should buy ... (p 16/1)
45. Dad told / wanted Ben to take the dog for a walk then. /
    Dad said to Ben that he should take the dog for a walk then. (p 16/2)
46. His secretary asked / told / advised / recommended / invited me to wait there until I was called /
    until they would call me / until they called me. (p 16/1, p 16/2)
47. Mr Smith asked / begged his son to cut the grass./
    Mr Smith said to his son that he should (be so kind as to) cut the grass. (p 16/1)
48. Mum advised / told / wanted Paul to go ... / Mum suggested that Paul should go ... (p 16/2)
49. Lucy asked / begged Mark to take her home then. /
    Lucy said to Mark that he should (be so kind as to) take her home then. (p 16/1)
50. Granny asked / told / wanted Laura to open the letter and (to) read what Mrs Johnson had written. (p 16/1, p 16/2)
51. The woman told / advised / recommended the boy to wait there until his mum came back. (p 16/2)
52. Mum said angrily to Joe that he should look what he had done. /
    Mum ordered / urged / shouted at / Joe to look what he had done. (p 17/3)
53. Dad asked / advised Bill to lock the door twice. /
    Dad said to Bill that he should (be so kind as to) lock the door twice. (p 16/1)
54. Mum said to Larry that he shouldn't use his fingers but eat with his ... /
    Mum told Larry not to use his fingers but eat with his ... (p 17/4, p 16/2)
55. Mum told / advised / wanted Tom to do his ... / Mum said to Tom that he should do ... /
    Mum suggested that Tom should do ... (p 16/2)
56. Mrs Manson allowed / asked / begged mum to keep the book as long as she wished./
    Mrs Manson said to mum that she should keep the book as long as she wished. (p 16/1)
57. Mum told Sue to wipe the ketchup off her mouth and fingers. /
    Mum said to Sue that she should wipe the ketchup off her mouth and fingers. (p 16/2)
58. Granny told Joe to wash his hands ... / Granny said to Joe that he should wash his hands ... (p 16/2)
59. Mum told / said to / dad that he shouldn't forget to buy ... / Mum told dad not to forget to buy ... (p 16/2, p17/4)
60. The policeman explained to me that I should take the first turning ... /
    The policeman told me to take the first turning ... (p 16/2)
61. The doctor advised / recommended / ordered me to remain in bed because I had got the flu. (p 16/2, p 17/3)
62. Mum advised / implored / told / wanted / ordered Tom to try to behave well. (p 16/1, p 16/2)
63. The doctor asked / invited Mrs Brown to take a seat / ... offered Mrs Brown a seat. (p 16/1)
64. Grandfather said to Jim that he should not / wasn't allowed to / interrupt him when he was speaking. /
    Grandfather ordered / commanded / wanted Jim not to interrupt him ... (p 17/3,4, p 16/2)
65. Nick advised / told / recommended Robert to tell her the truth. /
    Nick said to Robert that he should tell her the truth. (p 16/2)
66. Clare asked / begged / implored Eric not to leave her alone. (p 16/1, p 17/4)
67. Mum told / wanted / advised Pam to comb her hair and (to) change her shirt. /
    Mum said to Pam that she should comb her hair and change her shirt.(p 16/2)
68. Dad told / wanted / advised Bob to wipe the ketchup off his shirt./
    Dad said to Bob that he should wipe the ketchup off his shirt. (p 16/2)

69. Father told / wanted / his family to fasten their seat belts. /
Father said to his family that they should fasten their seat belts. (p 16/2)
70. Mum always tells / advises / wants / us to look both ways before we cross the street.
Mum always says to us that we should look both ways before we cross the street. (p 16/2)
71. Mrs Nigel asked / begged / implored / us not to smoke in there. / Mrs Nigel asked us very politely not to smoke in there. / Mrs Nigel asked us very politely that we shouldn't smoke in there. (p 16/1, p 17/4)
72. Mum said to Mrs Stone that she should have another slice of cake. / Mum invited Mrs Stone to (have) another slice of cake. / Mum insisted on (darauf bestehen) Mrs Stone('s) having another slice of cake. (p 16/1)
73. Mum ordered Bill not to lean ... / Mum wanted Bill not to lean ... /
Mum shouted at Bill that he shouldn't lean ... (p 17/3,4)
74. Mum advised / told / recommended granny to be careful and (to) mind the steps. /
Mum said to granny that she should be careful and mind the steps. (p 16/2)
75. The sign didn't allow picking flowers in the park. /
The sign said that picking flowers in the park wasn't allowed. (p 16/2, p 17/4)
76. Mum asked dad to buy a nice birthday present for his aunt. /
Mum said to dad that he should be so kind as to buy a nice ... (p 16/1)
77. The woman told the children to watch out because a car was coming. /
The woman said to the children that they should watch out because a car was coming. (p 16/2)
78. Mum told / wanted the children to go to bed <u>then</u>. /
Mum said to the children that they should go to bed <u>then</u>. (p 16/2)
79. Mrs Fisher invited me to have a cup of tea together. / Mrs Fisher suggested having ... / Mrs Fisher suggested that we had ... *Anmerkung: suggest kann nur mit that-Konstruktion oder dem Gerund stehen.* (p 16/2)
80. Mum warned / told / ordered / advised / recommended / Brian not to dye his hair blue because father would be angry. (p 17/4)
81. Stella asked / begged / reminded / me to call her at six. / Stella said to me that I should call her at six. (p16/1)
82. Dad advised / told / reminded / recommended / his friend to have a look at <u>that day's</u> newspaper because there was an interesting article in it. / Dad said to his friend that he should have a look at <u>that day's</u> newspaper because there was an interesting article in it. (p 16/2)
83. Mary and Ken suggested joining the drama club. / Mary and Ken suggested that we should join the drama club. *Anmerkung: suggest kann nur mit that-Konstruktion oder dem Gerund stehen.* (p 16/2)

pages 25, 26, 27

1. says / said / will say
2. tells / told / will tell
3. says / said / will say
4. told
5. says / said / will say
6. says / said / will say
7. tells / told / will tell
8. tells / told / will tell
9. tells / told / will tell
10. tells / told *(Zukunft nicht wegen Wortstellung)*
11. tell
12. tells / told
13. tells / told / will tell
14. tells / told / will tell
15. told
16. say
17. say
18. said
19. said
20. tells / told / will tell
21. tells / told / will tell
22. say
23. tell
24. say
25. saying
26. told
27. tells / told / will tell
28. saying
29. say
30. say
31. telling
32. tell
33. say
34. say
35. say
36. say
37. said, say
38. say
39. say
40. say
41. say
42. tells / told / will tell
43. told
44. said
45. say
46. Tell
47. say
48. tell
49. tell
50. told
51. tell
52. told
53. say, tell
54. saying
55. tell
56. tell
57. told
58. say, told
59. Tell
60. Tell, says / said / will say

61.	tells	91.	said
62.	tell	92.	told
63.	Tell	93.	tell
64.	says / said / will say	94.	Say
65.	told	95.	tells / told / will tell
66.	tell	96.	tell
67.	tell	97.	telling
68.	tell	98.	tell
69.	tell	99.	tell
70.	tell	100.	telling
71.	told	101.	says / said / will say
72.	telling	102.	told
73.	told	103.	said
74.	tell	104.	tell
75.	say, tells / told / will tell	105.	told
76.	say	106.	said
77.	say	107.	tells / told / will tell
78.	told	108.	told
79.	will tell	109.	says / said
80.	said (also see ☺ IV p 58)	110.	tell
81.	said	111.	said
82.	say	112.	saying
83.	Tell	113.	say
84.	said	114.	saying
85.	say	115.	tell
86.	tell	116.	say
87.	tells / told / will tell	117.	says / will say
88.	say	118.	Tell
89.	told	119.	tell
90.	tell, will tell		

pages 32, 33, 34

1. He left his bike / bicycle in the park.(☺ IV p 28 rule 2)
2. Let's leave it. (☺ IV p 28 rule 1)
3. Mother doesn't let him go to the p./ allow / permit him **to** go to the party. (☺ IV p 29 rule 3) (also see OBJECT WITH THE INFINITIVE with and without **to,** ☺ IV p 46,47)
4. Please leave the door open. (☺ IV p 28 rule 2)
5. That's all right! I'll invite you! (☺ IV p 31 rule 7)
6. Her husband left much unsaid. (☺ IV p 28 rule 2)
7. Please leave the key in the lock. (☺ IV p 28 rule 2)
8. He never lets us go on a holiday alone. / permits us to go / allows us to go (☺ IV p 29 rule 3) (also see infinitive with the object with and without **to,** (☺ IV p 46,47)
9. You can leave your coat here. (☺ IV p 28 rule 2)
10. Please leave me alone / leave me to myself (☺ IV p 28 rule 2) now and let me work (☺ IV p 29 rule 3)
11. You must leave two pages blank. (☺ IV p 28 rule 2)
12. He left her in the lurch / he let her down when she was having her baby.(☺ IV p 29 rule 4)
13. She didn't let the dog out of her sight. / She kept an eye on the dog. (☺ IV p 29 rule 4)
14. I am leaving it / that (up) to you if you come or not. (☺ IV p 28 rule 2)
15. You've left out number seven. (☺ IV p 28 rule 2)
16. He was ordered to rewrite the homework. (☺ IV p 29 rule 5) / They had him rewrite his homework. (☺ IV p 30 rule 6)
17. This film should make you think. (☺ IV p 29 rule 5)
18. The door doesn't open easily. (☺ IV p 31 rule 7)
19. His grandfather's death made him return. (☺ IV p 29 rule 5)
20. She had a new dress sewed. (☺ IV p 30 rule 6)
21. Your joke made everybody laugh. (☺ IV p 29 rule 5)
22. He should have his hair cut. (☺ IV p 30 rule 6)
23. The bad weather caused us to go farther south. / ... made us go ... (☺ IV p 29 rule 5)
24. She saw to it that the carpets were hoovered./ She ordered the carpets to be hoovered. (☺ IV p 29 rule 5) / She had the carpets hoovered. (☺ IV p 30 rule 6)
25. Leave the problems aside for a while. (☺ IV p 28 rule 2)
26. What, for Heaven's sake, made her leave her husband? (☺ IV p 29 rule 5)
27. What made him cry / weep? (☺ IV p 30 rule 6)
28. The beautiful weather made us take a walk / made us go for a walk. (☺ IV p 29 rule 5)

29. He had his bike cleaned. (☺ IV p 30 rule 6)
30. We'll **have to** (see: **modal verbs,** ☺ II p 7) have our room painted again. (☺ IV p 30 rule 6) / We must have our room painted again.
31. Tom has grown a beard. (☺ IV p 31 rule 7)
32. The doctor didn't keep us waiting very long. (☺ IV p 31 rule 7)
33. You may leave your hat on. (☺ IV p 28 rule 2)
34. She is letting up at school. (☺ IV p 29 rule 4)
35. They are having a greenhouse built in their garden. (☺ IV p 30 rule 6)
36. He left his purse / wallet in the shop. (☺ IV p 28 rule 2)
37. Nothing can be done about it. (☺ IV p 31 rule 7)
38. If you must, you must! (☺ IV p 31 rule 7)
39. He arranged for measures to be taken (in order) to help the refugees. / He ordered measures to be taken ... (☺ IV p 29 rule 5)
40. Robert didn't let the pretty girl out of his sight any more. (☺ IV p 29 rule 4)
41. She should have her coat cleaned. (☺ IV p 30 rule 6)
42. He is a great / splendid / excellent skier! We have got to give him that! (☺ IV p 31 rule 7)
43. Mrs Smith had her flat sold. (☺ IV p30 rule 6) / Mrs Smith arranged for her flat to be sold. (☺ IV p29 rule 5) / Mrs Smith saw to it that her flat was sold. (3. Lösung: sehr stakes Veranlassen: Sie setzte alles daran ...) (☺ IV p 29 rule 5)
44. Father had a tooth out. (☺ IV p 31 rule 7)
45. Father **had to** have a tooth out. (see: **modal verbs,** ☺ II p 7, ☺ IV p 30 rule 6)
46. I fear (that) we have left the light on. (☺ IV p 28 rule 2)
47. She was very sad but she didn't show anything.(*Achtung! Hier im Unterschied zum Deutschen nur Past Tense möglich! Handlung vergangen, kein Bezug zur Gegenwart.*) (☺ IV p 31 rule 7)
48. Mother was not to be persuaded (☺ IV p 31 rule 7) to let us go to the party. / ... to allow / to permit us to go ... . (☺ IV p 29 rule 3)
49. Please let him know (☺ IV p 31 rule 7) that I won't be lied to. (☺ IV p 31 rule 7)
50. You always leave your shoes about! (☺ IV p 28 rule 2)
51. He left his umbrella in the shop. (☺ IV p 28 rule 2)
52. We'll **have to** (see: **modal verbs,** ☺ II p 7) have the grass mowed. (☺ IV p 30 rule 6) / We'll have to arrange for the grass to be mowed. / We'll have to see to it that the grass is mowed. (☺ IV p 29 rule 5)
53. You should be made to think. (☺ IV p 29 rule 5)
54. I made him cry. (☺ IV p 29 rule 5)
55. You may leave your coat on. (☺ IV p 28 rule 2)
56. Please let us stay **with** Sarah overnight. / ... allow us to stay ... (☺ IV p 29 rule 3)
57. The snowstorm was letting up, so / that's why / therefore we could go out. (☺ IV p 29 rule 4)
58. She is a charming girl. We have got to give her that! (☺ IV p 31 rule 7)
59. After the (traffic) accident he left his car in the meadow. (☺ IV p 28 rule 2)
60. Please keep an eye on the oven. (☺ IV p 29 rule 4)
61. He needs your help! Don't leave him in the lurch now. / Don't let him down now. (☺ IV p 29 rule 4)
62. The wind is letting up. (☺ IV p 29 rule 4)
63. He had the TV turned down. (☺ IV p 30 rule 6)
64. You may leave the light on, if you are afraid. (☺ IV p 28 rule 2)
65. Please run water into the bath / tub. (☺ IV p 31 rule 7)
66. This sentence is not easy to translate. (☺ IV p 31 rule 7)
67. He loves gambling and leaves the casino with his pockets a lot lighter. (☺ IV p 31 rule 7)
68. People left the garbage on the road. (☺ IV p 28 rule 2)
69. You've left out one whole number. (☺ IV p 28 rule 2)
70. Please leave / keep your shoes on! (☺ IV p 28 rule 2)
71. I've left my shopping list at home. (☺ IV p 28 rule 2)
72. Leave that (up) to me. (☺ IV p 28 rule 2)
73. He left us at about seven. (☺ IV p 28 rule 2)
74. If you don't want to, then don't. (☺ IV p 28 rule 1)
75. Let's drop the whole idea. (☺ IV p 28 rule 1)
76. Please don't always leave your notebooks on the kitchen table. (☺ IV p 28 rule 2)
77. She dropped the vase. (☺ IV p 29 rule 4)
78. Can you come at eleven? – Yes, that's possible. / Yes, that can be done. (☺ IV p 31 rule 7)
79. She arranged for further measures to be taken against smoking in the office. (☺ IV p 29 rule 5)
80. He can't stop / keep from smoking. (☺ IV p 28 rule 1)
81. He can't help it. (☺ IV p 28 rule 1)
82. Let's leave it at that: We ('ll) meet at Jim's (place). (☺ IV p 28 rule 2)
83. Don't leave all your things about! (☺ IV p 28 rule 2)
84. Your handwriting leaves a lot to be desired. (☺ IV p 31 rule 7)
85. Simon was not to be persuaded to stay (any) longer. (☺ IV p 31 rule 7)
86. Let's go south. (☺ IV p 29 rule 3)
87. Allow me **to** stay out until / till midnight. / Let me stay out until ... (☺ IV p 29 rule 3)
88. He let the pupils go home one hour earlier. / He allowed / permitted the pupils **to** go ... (☺ IV p 29 rule 3)

89. Stop nagging! (☺ IV p 28 rule 1)
90. He can't stop climbing mountains. / He can't keep from climbing mountains. / He keeps on climbing ... / He cannot help climbing ... (☺ IV p 28 rule 1)
91. He must buy the latest computer. He can't help it. (☺ IV p 28 rule 1)
92. He can't stop playing tennis. / He can't keep from playing tennis. / He keeps on playing ... / He can't help playing ... (☺ IV p 28 rule 1)
93. He should leave it, if he doesn't want to. (☺ IV p 28 rule 1)
94. She can't help dating him again and again. (☺ IV p 28 rule 1)
95. Whenever she needs him, he leaves her in the lurch / he lets her down. (☺ IV p 29 rule 4)
96. Stop teasing her./ Leave off teasing her. (☺ IV p 28 rule 1)
97. He always makes his mother clear away his things. (☺ IV p 29 rule 5, *Anmerkung*: Regel 6 geht hier nicht, weil die Mutter als Ausführende genannt ist.)
98. I left my suitcase on the train. (☺ IV p 28 rule 2)
99. I won't let him get away with it. (☺ IV p 29 rule 3)
100. It was embarrassing that I kept them / her waiting. (☺ IV p 31 rule 7)
101. He is a looker. We have got to give him that. (☺ IV p 31 rule 7)
102. If you leave me alone now /
     If you leave me to myself now, I'll help you with the crossword puzzle later. (☺ IV p 28 rule 2)
103. Let's leave this aside now and let's concentrate on our homework. (☺ IV p 28 rule 2)
104. When we are on holiday we leave our mice with the neighbours. (☺ IV p 28 rule 2)
105. She left a short / brief message and left / went off / walked off. (☺ IV p 28 rule 2)
106. Don't bother about that. Leave that / it (up) / to me. (☺ IV p 29 rule 5)
107. Leave your gloves on, it's cold. (☺ IV p 29 rule 5)
108. Since she has been going steady with him she hasn't let him out of her sight / she has been keeping an eye on him. (☺ IV p 29 rule 4)
109. How about a bike tour? The rain is letting up. (☺ IV p 29 rule 4)
110. She likes dating Bill. He always makes her laugh. (☺ IV p 29 rule 5)
111. Watch out!/ Be careful! Don't drop the cup! (☺ IV p 29 rule 4)
112. The thunderstorm made her / them stay at home. (☺ IV p 29 rule 5)
113. He is having the old sofa taken away. (☺ IV p 30 rule 6)
114. She let herself be kissed under the tree. (☺ IV p 29 rule 3)
115. The teacher made us write a book report. / ... caused us to write ... / ... saw to it that we wrote ... / ordered us to write ... (☺ IV p 29 rule 5) *Anmerkung: Befehlsempfänger genannt.*
116. The teacher had a book report written. (☺ IV p 30 rule 6) *Anmerkung: Befehlsempfänger nicht genannt.*
117. They saw to it that he arranged for measures to be taken. (☺ IV p 29 rule 5)
118. Michael shouldn't always leave his umbrella just anywhere. (☺ IV p 28 rule 2)
119. He had his hair dyed orange. (☺ IV p 30 rule 6)
120. When he dates Sally she always keeps him waiting for a long time. (☺ IV p 31 rule 7)
121. We left the radio on. Please go and turn it off. (☺ IV p 28 rule 2)
122. Barbara was not to be persuaded to visit him. (☺ IV p 31 rule 7)
123. Can you put away the shoes? – Yes, that's possible. / that can be done. (☺ IV p 31 rule 7)
124. The tin / can (American English) opens easily. (☺ IV p 31 rule 7) /The tin can be opened easily.

page 42

1. to (☺ IV p 35/1)
2. X (☺ IV p 40/1)
3. X (☺ IV p 41/3)
4. X (☺ IV p 40/2)
5. to (☺ IV p 37/4)
6. to (☺ IV p 36/3)
7. to (☺ IV p 36/3), to (☺ IV p 35/1)
8. X (☺ IV p 40/1), to (☺ IV p 36/3)
9. X (☺ IV p 40/2)
10. to (☺ IV p 36/3)
11. to (☺ IV p 35/1), X (☺ IV p 41/4)
12. to (☺ IV p 35/1)
13. to (☺ IV p 38/9)
14. To (☺ IV p 38/10)
15. to (☺ IV p 37/4)
16. to (☺ IV p 40/1)
17. to (☺ IV p 35/2), X, X (☺ IV p 41/4)
18. to (☺ IV p 37/4), (to) (☺ IV p 37/4)
19. to (☺ IV p 35/2)
20. to (☺ IV p 35/1), (☺ IV p 39/11)
21. to (☺ IV p 35/2)
22. to (☺ IV p 39/12)
23. to (☺ IV p 35/2)
24. to (☺ IV p 37/4), to (☺ IV p 35/1), to (☺ IV p 38/8), (to) (☺ IV p 48/3)
25. X (☺ IV p 41/3)
26. to, X (☺ IV p 41/4)
27. to (☺ IV p 35/1)
28. to (☺ IV p 40/1)
29. to (☺ IV p 40/1)
30. to (☺ IV p 39/11)
31. X (☺ IV p 41/3)
32. To (☺ IV p 38/10), X (☺ IV p 40/1)
33. to (☺ IV p 37/6)
34. to (☺ IV p 38/9)
35. (to) (☺ IV p 40/1)
36. to (☺ IV p 38/7)
37. X, X (☺ IV p 40/2)

page 45

1. The girl to come to Peter's party is Linda Jones.
2. He was the first man to swim across the Atlantic.
3. I need someone to show me how the computer works.
4. He still has some exams to pass.
5. You really haven't got anything to complain about.
6. I need a brush to clean your coat with.
7. It was great to hear that he had won the first prize.
8. I am very sorry to have to say that we can't trust him.
9. Could you please draw a plan of how to find your house?
10. She explained to Sue how to use the typewriter.
11. He was not sure how long to stay with us.
12. Can you tell us where to find you?
13. We wondered where to go next.
14. There is no interesting book in the hotel library (for me) to read.
15. Frank is the only person (for me) to tell my secrets.
16. She has decided not to leave him.
17. He is not sure to arrive at three.
18. He explained (to me) how to repair the car.
19. He decided not to visit her any more.
20. I'd be happy to help you.
21. Robert and I haven't got anything to talk about.
22. Have you decided which hat to buy?
23. This is an important question (for us) to answer.
24. I need new coloured pencils to draw with.
25. They are certain to try to attract attention.
26. I still have got some presents to wrap up.
27. I'd be very pleased to meet him.
28. Mrs Grant was the next person to arrive.
29. There was no interesting film (for you) to watch on TV.
30. I asked how to get to the airport the fastest.
31. The most important question (for me) is what to do next.
32. We are certain to meet her in our holidays.
33. It is very dangerous to stretch your arm out of the window.
34. He followed Linda to see her enter Joe's flat, which made him sad.
35. He was too fast for us to catch him.
36. I asked when to leave.
37. The problem is how to find a nice present for Jim.
38. The desk is too heavy for her to move it.

pages 50, 51

1. to (p 46/1)
2. to (p 46/1)
3. X (p 47/2)
4. to (p 46/1)
5. (to) (p 48/3)
6. to (p 46/1)
7. to (p 46/1)
8. to (p 46/1)
9. to (p 48/3)
10. X (p 47/2)
11. to (p 46/1)
12. to (p 46/1)
13. to (p 46/1)
14. X (p 47/2)
15. (to) (p 48/3)
16. to (p 46/1)
17. to (p 48/3)
18. X (p 47/2)
19. X (p 47/2)
20. to (p 46/1)
21. X (p 47/2)
22. to (p 46/1)
23. to (p 46/1)
24. to (p 48/4)
25. to (p 46/1)
26. X, X (p 47/2)
27. to (p 46/1, p 47, negative infinitive)
28. to (p 46/1)
29. to (p 46/1)
30. X (p 47/2)
31. X (p 47/2)
32. X (p 47/2)
33. X (p 47/2)
34. to (p 46/1, p 47, negative infinitive)
35. to (p 46/1)
36. to (p 46/1)
37. to (p 46/1)
38. to (p 46/1, p 47, negative infinitive)
39. to (p 46/1)
40. X (p 47/2)
41. X (p 47/2)
42. X (p 47/2)
43. to (p 46/1)
44. to (p 48/3)
45. X (p 47/2)
46. to (p 46/1)
47. to (p 46/1, p 47, negative infinitive)
48. to (p 46/1)
49. to (p 48/3)
50. to (p 46/1, p 47, negative infinitive)
51. to (p 46/1)
52. X (p 47/2)
53. (to) (p 48/3)
54. to (p 46/1)
55. to (p 49/5)
56. to (p 46/1)
57. to (p 46/1)
58. to (p 46/1, p 47, negative infinitive)
59. to (p 46/1)
60. to (p 46/1)
61. X (p 47/2)
62. to (p 46/1)
63. to (p 46/1, p 47, negative infinitive)
64. X (p 47/2)
65. to (p 46/1)
66. to (p 46/1)
67. to (p 46/1)
68. to (p 46/1)
69. to (p 46/1)
70. to (p 46/1)
71. to (p 46/1, p 47, negative infinitive)
72. X (p 47/2)
73. to (p 46/1)
74. to (p 46/1)
75. X (p 47/2)
76. to (p 46/1)
77. to (p 46/1)
78. to (p 46/1)
79. to (p 46/1)

page 52

1. I want you to help me in the garden. (☺ IV p 46/1)
2. He suggested that I should eat less sugar and fat. (☺IV p16, p48/3)
3. She prefers to stay at home today. (☺ IV p 35/1, p 73/2)
4. Dad ordered me to mow the grass and to take Rex for a walk. (☺ IV p 46/1)
5. I would like you to stop smoking. (☺ IV p 46/1)
6. You can't force her to become an interpreter if she doesn't want to. (☺ IV p 46/1)
7. I always thought him to be an honest man. (☺ IV p 46/1)
8. He told me to believe in success. (☺ IV p 46/1)
9. He didn't allow us to try the miracle drug. (☺ IV p 46/1)
10. I must remember to buy flowers. (☺ IV p 46/1, p 74/3)
11. She persuaded us to give up playing basketball. (☺ IV p 46/1)
12. I think her to be very friendly. (☺ IV p 46/1)
13. I don't want you to eat so much sweet stuff. (☺ IV p 46/1)
14. He explained how to bake bread. (☺ IV p 38/9)
15. He asked me to throw away the waste. (☺ IV p 46/1)
16. I want him to come home. (☺ IV p 46/1)
17. He doesn't want us to be late. (☺ IV p 46/1)
18. Please show me how to swing the tennis racket. (☺ IV p 46/1)
19. Please remind me to turn down the TV. (☺ IV p 46/1)
20. He persuaded her to become a vegetarian. (☺ IV p 46/1)
21. We saw him come home drunk. (☺ IV p 47/2)
22. Could you help me (to) carry the parcel? (☺ IV p 48/3)
23. He made us train hard for the competition. (☺ IV p 47/2)
24. We suggested that she should stay with us overnight. (☺ IV p 16, p 48/3)
25. You always make us laugh. (☺ IV p 47/2)
26. We were not heard to sing. (☺ IV p 48/3)
27. He was let go after paying the bill. (☺ IV p 48/3)
28. I don't want you to take loads of whipped cream. (☺ IV p 46/1)
29. I told him when to meet. (☺ IV p 48/4)
30. She never knows what to say. (☺ IV p 48/4)
31. He isn't sure which trousers to put on. (☺ IV p 48/4)
32. He didn't tell us who to invite. (☺ IV p 48/4)
33. Fred always tells her what to think and what to do. (☺ IV p 48/4)
34. Can you tell me where to look for my umbrella? (☺ IV p 48/4)
35. I would like her to learn French. (☺ IV p 46/1)
36. I suggested that he should take my car. (☺ IV p 16, p 48/3)

pages 56, 57

1. be taken (☺ IV p 53/2)
2. be solved (☺ IV p 53/2)
3. be written (☺ IV p 53/2)
4. read (☺ IV p 55/4a)
5. be blamed (☺ IV p 53/1) / auch: to blame
6. be answered (☺ IV p 53/1)
7. be sold (☺ IV p 53/1)
8. be done / do (☺ IV p 54/3a)
9. eat / be eaten (☺ IV p 54/3b)
10. eat (☺ IV p 55/4b)
11. be sent (☺ IV p 53/2)
12. be stolen (☺ IV p 53/2)
13. be written (☺ IV p 53/1)
14. to drink / to be drunk (☺ IV p 54/3b)
15. paid (☺ IV p 53/2)
16. be heard (☺ IV p 53/2)
17. be handed (☺ IV p 53/2)
18. be given (☺ IV p 53/2)
19. be pitied (☺ IV p 53/1)
20. be desired (☺ IV p 53/1)
21. be listened (☺ IV p 53/2)
22. be sold (☺ IV p 53/1)
23. be done (☺ IV p 53/1)
24. let (☺ IV p 55/4d)
25. pass (☺ IV p 54/4b)
26. pass / be passed (☺ IV p 54/3b)
27. pass (☺ IV p 55/4a)
28. be loved (☺ IV p 53/2)
29. be left (☺ IV p 53/1)
30. be fired (☺ IV p 53/2)
31. be read (☺ IV p 53/2)
32. be opened (☺ IV p 53/2) / auch: will open
33. be left (☺ IV p 53/1)
34. be cleaned (☺ IV p 53/2)
35. be solved (☺ IV p 53/2)
36. be kissed (☺ IV p 53/2)
37. be invited (☺ IV p 53/1)
38. be picked (☺ IV p 53/2)
39. be talked (☺ IV p 53/1)
40. read (☺ IV p 55/4c)
41. drink (☺ IV p 55/4a)
42. reach (☺ IV p 55/4a)
43. reach / be reached (☺ IV p 54/3b)
44. reach (☺ IV p 55/4b)
45. write (☺ IV p 55/4a)
46. invite / be invited (☺ IV p 54/3b)
47. invite (☺ IV p 55/4b)
48. answer / be answered (☺ IV p 54/3a)
49. be told (☺ IV p 53/2)
50. be found (☺ IV p 53/1)
51. be sold (☺ IV p 53/1)
52. be done / do (☺ IV p 54/3a)
53. be taken (☺ IV p 53/2)
54. smell (☺ IV p 55/4a)
55. be desired (☺ IV p 53/1)
56. be put (☺ IV p 53/2)
57. answer (☺ IV p 55/4a)
58. answer / be answered (☺ IV p 54/3b)
59. answer (☺ IV p 55/4b)
60. be left (☺ IV p 53/1)
61. be mended (☺ IV p 53/2)
62. look (☺ IV p 55/4a)
63. eat / be eaten (☺ IV p 54/3b)
64. lose / be lost (☺ IV p 54/3a)
65. understand (☺ IV p 55/4a)

66. carry / be carried (☺ IV p 54/3b)
67. carry (☺ IV p 55/4b)
68. carry (☺ IV p 55/4a)
69. be cleaned (☺ IV p 53/2)
70. talk (☺ IV p 55/4c)
71. drink (☺ IV p 55/4a)
72. eat / be eaten (☺ IV p 54/3b)
73. ride (☺ IV p 55/4a)
74. be found (☺ IV p 53/1)
75. be seen (☺ IV p 53/1)
76. be seen (☺ IV p 53/1)
77. be sold (☺ IV p 53/1)
78. do / be done (☺ IV p 54/3a)
79. be asked (☺ IV p 53/2)

page 60

Mehrere Lösungen sind möglich. Hier eine Auswahl:

1. People say / It is said / that they share / are sharing a room.
2. Mr Schneider is supposed to be very rich.
3. They believe / People believe / It is believed / that Mrs Miller nags her husband.
4. They thought / People thought / It was thought / that he would come back.
5. They found / People found / that he was very strange. / They found him very strange.
6. It is reported that she won in the lottery.
7. They know / People know / It is known / that he lost his father in a boating accident.
8. They didn't think / People didn't think / It wasn't thought / that he would help her.
9. The house is supposed to be haunted.
10. They considered visiting him on Friday *(see gerund)*.
11. They say / People say / It is said / that he is a friendly teacher. / He is said to be a friendly teacher.
12. They think / People think / It is thought / that Mr Stone will sell his car./ Mr Stone is thought to be selling his car.
13. They supposed / People supposed / It was supposed / that he would run away.
14. They know / People know / It is known / that he will buy a house. / He is known to be buying a house.
15. They believe / People believe / It is believed / that they are divorced. / They are believed to be divorced.
16. They reported / People reported / It was reported / that he had won the first prize. / He was reported to have won the first prize.
17. It is believed that the house was built in the 16th century.
18. They didn't think / People didn't think / It wasn't thought / that the girl was still alive. / The girl wasn't thought to be still alive.
19. They supposed / People supposed / It was supposed / that he wouldn't be there.
20. They claimed / People claimed / It was claimed / that he was very jealous.
21. Shi Xu Xi is believed to be the oldest man in the world.
22. They report / People report / It is reported / that the war is over./The war is reported to be over.
23. They claim / People claim / It is claimed / that he is a good father.
24. The stolen ring is reported to be worth more than 5000 pounds.
25. They didn't believe / People didn't believe / It wasn't believed / that he was able to run (that he could run) so fast. / He wasn't believed to be able to run so fast.
26. „Schindlers List" is said to be one of Spielberg's best films.
27. They said / People said / It was said / that he loved children very much. / He was said to have loved children very much.
28. They didn't find / People didn't find / that the exam was difficult. / The exam wasn't found to be difficult.
29. They thought / People thought / It was thought / that Maria had got to know her husband in Vienna. / Maria was thought to have got to know her husband in Vienna.
30. They say / People say / It is said / that he has a new girl-friend./ He is said to have a new girl-friend.
31. They know / People know / It is known / that Charlie is fond of cooking. / Charlie is known to be fond of cooking.
32. They supposed / People supposed / It was supposed / that he had stolen the money.
33. They think / People think / It is thought / that Laura was ill. / Laura is thought to have been ill.
34. They claim / People claim / It is claimed / that Mr Jones is in hospital./ Mr Jones is claimed to be in hospital.
35. They reported / People reported / It was reported / that he was (had been) very sad. / He was reported to have been very sad.
36. The ship was reported missing.
37. They understand / People understand / It is understood that he is so excited. / They understand his (him) being so excited *(see gerund)*.
38. They suppose / People suppose / It is supposed / that he will get married soon.
39. They knew / People knew / It was known / that he wouldn't stay long.
40. They said / People said / It was said / that Frank had been in America for a long time. / Frank was said to have been in America for a long time.

pages 70, 71, 72

1. of driving (p 66/5)
2. to spending (p 66/5)
3. at meeting (p 67/6)
4. up smoking (p 66/5)
5. about eating (p 67/6)
6. of buying (p 66/5)
7. on visiting (p 66/5)
8. at / about not finding (p 67/6)
9. of listening to (p 67/6)
10. of driving (p 67/6)
11. on working (p 67/6)
12. at not quarrelling (p 67/6)
13. against his becoming (*written, formal English*) / against him becoming (*spoken English*) (p 66/5)
14. against smoking (p 66/5)
15. to his flirting (*written, formal English*) / to him flirting (*spoken English*) (p 66/5)
16. (in) talking (p 68/7)
17. for baking (p 67/6)
18. to working (p 67/6)
19. (in) complaining (p 68/7)
20. for / about not calling (p 67/6)
21. to getting (p 67/6)
22. (in) keeping (p 68/7)
23. of treating (p 68/7)
24. about / at (p 67/6) the pupils' preparing (*written, formal English*) / the pupils preparing (*spoken English*) Keep in mind: I'm pleased **to meet** you.
25. of falling (p 68/7)
26. of travelling (p 68/7)
27. about his being (p 68/7) (*written, formal English*)/ him being (*spoken English*)
28. of crying (p 68/7)
29. of winning (p 67/6)
30. at / about meeting (p 67/6)
31. about (p 67/6) his behaving (*written, formal English*) / him behaving (*spoken English*)
32. for complaining (p 68/7)
33. on winning (p 66/5)
34. about visiting (p 67/6)
35. (in) finding (p 68/7)
36. to drinking (p 66/5)
37. for her leaving (p 68/7)
38. from working (müde sein) / of working (es satt haben) (p 67/6)
39. for being (p 66/5)
40. with being (p 66/5)
41. about quarrelling (p 66/5)
42. on working (p 66/5)
43. about being (p 67/6)
44. in sailing (p 68/7)
45. at not meeting (p 67/6)
46. in escaping (p 66/5)
47. on my being (*written, formal English*) / on me being (*spoken English*) (p 66/5)
48. from leaving (p 66/5)
49. at climbing (p 67/6)
50. of being (p 86)
51. of helping (p 67/6)
52. of having (p 67/6)
53. about going (p 66/5)
54. to stealing / to having stolen (p 66/5)
55. to doing (p 67/6)
56. of having (p 66/5)
57. of working / to work (p 68/7)
58. in thinking (p 67/6)
59. (in) finding (p 68/7)
60. of my staying (*written*) / of me staying (*spoken*) (p 66/5)
61. of moving (p 66/5)
62. from believing (p 67/6)
63. in making (p 68/7)
64. of meeting (p 68/7)
65. of doing (p 67/6)
66. in listening (p 67/6)
67. in thinking (p 67/6)
68. of being (p 67/6)
69. to his spending (*written*) / to him spending (*spoken*) (p 66/5)
70. on her not driving (p 66/5), of her damaging (p 67/6)
71. (in) getting a good job (p 68/7)
72. of booking (p 68/7)
73. to / in / of knowing (p 68/7)
74. about / at his being (*written*) / about / at him being (*spoken*) (p 67/6)
75. by Mr Miller's being (*written*) / by Mr Miller being (*spoken*) (p 67/6)
76. (of) trying (p 68/7)
77. for / about forgetting (p 67/6)
78. to walking (p 68/7)
79. at handling (p 67/6)
80. up with working (p 67/6)
81. about / at his bringing (*written*) / about / at him bringing (*spoken*) (p 67/6)
82. of going (p 68/7)
83. on my helping (*written*) / on me helping (*spoken*) (p 66/5)
84. off teasing (p 66/5)
85. for your helping (*written*) / for you helping (*spoken*) (p 67/6)
86. of her drinking (p 66/5)
87. to reading (p 66/5)
88. by mowing (p 66/5)
89. for throwing (p 66/5)
90. between going (p 68/7)
91. of talking (p 68/7)
92. for leaving (p 68/7)
93. of telling (p 68/7)
94. of starting (p 68/7)
95. of driving (p 66/5)
96. on our doing (*written*) / on us doing (*spoken*) (p 66/5)
97. to visiting (p 66/5)
98. with caring (p 66/5)
99. on talking (p 66/5)

pages 78 – 83

1. having (p 64/4)
2. being (p 64/4)
3. to invite (p 35/1)
4. going (p 64/4)
5. saying (p 64/4)
6. saying (p 64/4)
7. being (p 64/4)
8. going (p 64 /4)
9. to go (p 35/1)
10. going (p 66/5)
11. to meet (p 35/1)
12. doing (p 69/8)
13. shouting (p 64/4)
14. getting (p 64/4)
15. being (p 63/2, 64/4)
16. finding (p 68/7)
17. to give (p 48/3)
18. doing (p 66/5)
19. making (p 63/2, p 64/4)
20. to understand (p 73/1/ Attention)
21. finding (p 67/6)
22. to hear (p 35/2)
23. to go / going (p 64/4, p 73/1)
24. working (p 69/8)
25. telling (p 69/8)
26. make (p 47/2)
27. visiting (p 69/8)
28. smoking (p 66/5)
29. to join (p 73/2)
30. leave (p 40/2)
31. to send (p 74/3)
32. to get (p 35/1)
33. give (p 47/2), smoking (p 63/1)
34. to dance (p 73/2)
35. to pick (p 35/1)
36. hurting (p 74/3)
37. talking (p 76/6), to listen to (p 73/2)
38. to catch (p 77/8) *versuchen = sich bemühen*
39. telling (p 74/3)
40. reading (p 73/2), to watch (p 73/2)
41. to talk (p 76/6)
42. being (p 64/4)
43. to keep (p 46/1)
44. listening (p 64/4)
45. catch (p 47/2)
46. making (p 64/4, 73/2)
47. to tell (p 74/3) **remember** is the first action, it refers to the **future**, watering (p 75/5)
48. to be (p 46/1)
49. speaking (p 64/4)
50. take (p 40/2)
51. telling (p 64/4)
52. going (p 73/2)
53. to see (p 35/1)
54. lying (p 64/4)
55. finding (p 74/3) **remember** is the second action, referring to the **past**
56. playing (p 73/2)
57. to walk (p 73/2)
58. getting (p 66/5)
59. to go (p 36/3)
60. drinking (p 77/8) *try = ausprobieren*
61. saying (p 64/4)
62. leaving (p 66/5)
63. to pick up (p 76/6)
64. to visit (p 76/6), seeing (p 69/8)
65. to go (p 36/3)
66. turning (p 64/4)
67. asking (p 69/8)
68. interrupting (p 69/8)
69. seeing (p 69/8)
70. to go (p 36/3)
71. flirting (p 64/4)
72. looking (p 74/3) **remember** is the second action, referring to the **past**
73. filling (p 64/4)
74. seeing (p 64/4)
75. to go (p 35/2), waiting (p 64/4)
76. stealing / having stolen (p 64/4)
77. to say (p 36/3)
78. leave (p 40/2)
79. show (p 47/2)
80. becoming (p 63/3)
81. sleeping (p 68/7)
82. fishing (p 67/6)
83. to get (p 76/6)
84. playing (p 64/4)
85. to leave (p 36/3)
86. drinking (p 64/4, p 73/2)
87. to meet (p 35/1), being (p 64/4)
88. disturbing (p 67/6), working (p 76/6)
89. to play (p 36/3) / for playing (p 68/7)
90. to write (p 74/3) **forget** is the first action, it refers to the **future**,
91. climbing (p 69/8)
92. to leave (p 36/3)
93. to spend (p 46/1)
94. to explain (p 74/3) **forget** is the first action, it refers to the **future**, bringing (p 64/4)
95. painting (p 75/5)
96. saying (p 74/3) **remember** is the second action, referring to the **past**
97. to fall (p 37/4)
98. to get (p 74/3) **forget** is the first action, it refers to the **future**
99. using (p 67/6), asking (p 86)
100. trying (p 69/8), to move (p 46/1)
101. to complain (p 37/4)
102. thinking (p 67/6)
103. being (p 67/6)
104. to spend (p 37/5)
105. behaving (p 76/6)
106. paying (p 74/3)
107. getting (p 64/4, p 73/2)
108. to wash (p 74/3)
109. dyeing (p 75/5)
110. giving (p 74/3) **regret** is the second action, referring to the **past**
111. ask / to ask (p 40/1)
112. to smoke (p 46/1, p 73/2)
113. being (p 67/6)
114. to drink (p 73/2)
115. reading (p 73/2)
116. ride (p 40/2), practise (p 40/2), playing (p 64/4)
117. reading (p 64/4, p 73/2)
118. to help (p 77/8)
119. to get (p 46/1)
120. staying (p 73/2), going (p 73/2)

121. returning (p 74/3)
122. to read (p 73/2)
123. to stop (p 46/1), smoking (p 76/6), smoking (p 73/2) *Befehlsempfänger ist nicht genannt, daher allgemeine Aussage*
124. shouting (p 76/6)
125. to climb (p 73/2) *Befehlsempfänger ist genannt, daher spezielle Situation*
126. laughing (p 69/8)
127. to go (p 73/2) *spezielle Situation mit would love*
128. having (p 73/2) *Befehlsempfänger ist nicht genannt, daher allgemeine Aussage*
129. to stay (p 73/2)
130. to stay (p 73/2)
131. to be (p 46/1)
132. to tell (p 73/2) *dass ich dir ... sagen muss*
133. hoovering (p 75/5)
134. to leave (p 46/1, p 73/2)
135. saying (p 74/3) *dass sie gesagt hat /* to say (p 74/3) *dass sie sagen muss*
136. knitting (p 73/2)
137. to stay (p 46/1)
138. to hurt (p 75/4), to make (p 35/1), cry (p 47/2)
139. to have (p 76/6)
140. writing (p 77/8) *try = ausprobieren,* writing (p 66/5)
141. to eat (p 46/1)
142. to call (p 46/1)
143. leaving (p 67/6)
144. to persuade (p 77/8) *try = sich bemühen,* to give up (p 46/1), smoking (p 66/5)
145. moving (p 74/3)
146. to forget (p 73/2) *spezielle Situation*
147. to call (p 74/3) **forget** *is the first action, it refers to the future*
148. watching (p 73/2), having (p 67/6)
149. to have (p 73/2) *spezielle Situation mit* would like
150. whisper (p 47/2)
151. working (p 76/6)
152. to eat (p 73/2) *Befehlsempfänger ist erwähnt*
153. to come (p 48/3) / coming / to have come
154. having (p 73/2)
155. changing (p 75/5)
156. to steal (p 48/3) / stealing
157. to wipe (p 46/1)
158. to pick up (p 74/3) **forget** *is the first action, it refers to the future*
159. allowing (p 74/3) **remember** *is the second action, referring to the* **past***,* to use (p 46/1)
160. tidy (p 47/2)
161. cleaning (p 75/5), to take (p 74/3) **forget** *is the first action, it refers to the future, dass du den Mantel hinbringen musst*
162. to get (p 76/6)
163. to have (p 73/2) *spezielle Situation mit* would love, meeting (p 68/7)
164. to explain (p 76/7) *und dann erklärte er /* explaining (p 76/7) *er erklärte sie uns* weiter
165. oiling (p 75/5)
166. cleaning (p 75/4)
167. study (p 47/2)
168. getting up (p 73/2), going (p 73/2)
169. cleaning (p 75/5)
170. complaining (p 69/8)
171. reading (p 63/1)
172. sweat (p 47/2)
173. inviting (p 64/4)
174. being (p 64/4)
175. drinking (p 64/4)
176. to reach (p 43)
177. calling (p 64/4)
178. being (p 64/4)
179. talking (p 64/4)
180. forgetting (p 63/2) (p 64/4)
181. ironing (p 68/7), helping (p 67/6)
182. knowing (p 69/8)
183. hanging (p 69/8), doing (p 69/8)
184. reading (p 76/7)
185. tremble (p 47/2)
186. to win (p 77/8) *try = sich bemühen*
187. sleeping (p 64/4) *(hier fancy = etwas gerne tun)*
188. to meet (p 35/1)
189. cut (p 47/2)

page 85

1. drinking
2. getting
3. be
4. living
5. being
6. taking
7. like
8. watch
9. wear
10. cooking, doing, ironing
11. be
12. go
13. be
14. going
15. drink
16. smoke
17. having
18. go
19. driving
20. get
21. live
22. be

page 88

1. Instead of complaining try to work harder.
2. He is angry with me for calling him a liar.
3. He went away without taking his umbrella with him.
4. By trying hard you will win.
5. I don't use my comp. for writing personal letters.
6. She earns some money by doing silk painting.
7. I must thank you for paying back the m. in time.
8. He was able to escape the police by jumping out of the window.
9. She suggested going to the cinema.
10. After finding a nice B&B we went to bed. *(bei **after** ziehen wir finding einem having found vor).*
11. On meeting him I gave him my address.
12. The boy denied having stolen / denied stealing her purse.
13. I cannot understand Simon('s) being so angry.
14. He greeted her without looking into her eyes.
15. Her eyes were red with weeping.
16. Before going to bed he closed the window.
17. In spite of having everything he wanted Sam was unhappy.
18. Before having my breakfast I usually take a shower.
19. After getting a bad mark he decided to study harder. *(bei **after** ziehen wir getting einem having got vor.)*
20. He is depressed about not having a job.
21. Billy ran across the road without looking.
22. Lilly was afraid of the cat('s) scratching her.
23. Do you **mind my** *(written English)* opening / **me** opening *(spoken English)* the window for a moment? *(2 verschiedene Subjekte)* (p86/2, p64/4)
24. I still **remember** falling in love for the first time (p 74/3)
25. By being so loud you will wake up the baby.
26. I have got special scissors for cutting metal as well as cloth.
27. After finishing lunch he took a nap. *(bei **after** ziehen wir finishing einem having finished vor.)*
28. In spite of eating very little Frank is rather fat.
29. Instead of hanging around you should read a good book.
30. On arriving in Paris we phoned our friends.
31. You will get some extra pocket money by mowing Mr Spencer's lawn.
32. Before entering the house he emptied the letter b.
33. I want to give him a little present for being so kind to us.
34. After winning the game he was exhausted. *(bei **after** ziehen wir winning einem having won vor.)*
35. Sandy is unhappy at having to remain in bed. (must = have to, ☺ II p 7)
36. Instead of going home he went to a bar.
37. He doesn't **mind our** *(written English)* inviting / **us** inviting *(spoken English)* Robert to our party. *(2 verschiedene Subjekte)* (p 86/2, p 64/4)
38. Instead of watching TV all day she should help in the garden.
39. I still **remember his** arriving *(written English)*/ **him** arriving *(spoken English)*. *(2 verschiedene Subjekte)* (p 86/2)
40. After eating lots of whipped cream I felt sick. *(bei **after** ziehen wir eating einem having eaten vor.)*

page 89

1. lock (☺ III p 7/1)
2. would leave (☺ III p 9)
3. will miss (☺ III p 7/2)
4. was / were (☺ III p 9)
5. would not be (☺ III p 65/1)
6. need (☺ III p 7)
7. had not been (☺ III p 65/2)
8. had gone (☺ III p 65/2)
9. wouldn't be (☺ III p 65/1)
10. would be (☺ III p 9)
11. hadn't helped (☺ III p 65/2)
12. will be worried (☺ III p 7/2)
13. would be (☺ III p 9)
14. would have missed (☺ III p 65/2)
15. mustn't (☺ III p 7/2)

*

1. (that/which) (☺ III p 79/2)
   4. Fall kann ausgelassen werden
2. whose (☺ III p 78/1)
3. who/that (☺ III p 78/1)
4. (that/which) (☺ III p 79/2) *Relativpronomen vor Präposition kann ausgelassen werden; entspricht dem deutschen 3. Fall*
5. (who/that) (☺ III p 78/1)
   4. Fall kann ausgelassen werden
6. (that/which) (☺ III p 79/2)
   4. Fall kann ausgelassen werden
7. that/which (☺ III p 79/2), *1.Fall*
8. which (☺ III p 81/4)
9. What (☺ III p 81/5)
10. (that) (☺ III p 80/3a)

page 94

1. The old man was sitting on a bench sleeping. /
   The old man sitting on a bench was sleeping.
2. Having taken a seat he ordered a pint of beer.
3. Having eaten they cleared the table.
4. Feeling rather exhausted I lay down a bit.
5. She was lying on the floor writing her diary. /
   Lying on the floor she was writing her diary.
6. Is there anybody wishing to talk to me?
7. Mrs Brown was on her way home talking to herself.
8. Reading a book in bed I fell asleep.
9. Having written the letter she took it to the post office.
10. Not knowing his phone number she couldn't call him.
11. We saw some people swimming in the cold river.
12. Arriving I noticed a policeman standing behind my car.
13. Having bought some food we began to cook.
14. She entered the room smiling at everybody. /
    Entering the room she smiled at everybody.
15. Running after the bus he lost his key.
16. I watched the little girl picking flowers.
17. Preparing dinner *mum* cut herself.

18. Having drunk too much wine Peter felt sick.
19. The boys waiting in front of the school are Sally's friends.
20. I saw Bob kissing Barbara.
21. Having come in Bill took off his shoes.
22. He fell down hitting his head on the floor.
23. Knowing that she might lose she gave up.
24. Jumping into the pond Tom lost his bathing trunks.
25. Being a good swimmer Simon won the competition.
26. We felt the house shaking.
27. He came in greeting us politely. / Coming in he greeted us politely.
28. Having done all the ironing Mr Spencer lit his pipe.
29. Fearing that the police might find his gun he hid it in the shed.
30. Not knowing how to interpret the poem she was silent.
31. Drinking from her mug she burnt her lips.
32. Time rushing along we had to run in order to catch our train.
33. The weather being very nice we decided to go on a trip. *(two different subjects)*
34. Having read the brochures he chose to go to Ireland that summer.
35. Approaching the house we saw that a window had been broken.
36. Asking her father Sue hoped he would know the answer. / Sue asked her father hoping he …
37. Not having eaten a good breakfast she was hungry.
38. He rushed out of the room slamming the door.
39. The train standing on platform four goes to Vienna.
40. The woman got out of the bus carrying two heavy bags./ The woman getting out of the bus carried two heavy bags.
41. He thought about the answer biting his lips. / Thinking about the answer he bit his lips.

SMILE
READING COMPREHENSIONS

Sinnerfassendes Lesen ist im Unterricht jetzt ein ganz großes Thema. Kinder sollen trainieren, so aufmerksam zu lesen, dass sie den Sinn des Gelesenen erfassen und verwerten können.

ISBN 978-3-7074-1354-0   ISBN 978-3-7074-1508-7   ISBN 978-3-7074-1624-4   ISBN 978-3-7074-1846-0

SMILE READING COMPREHENSIONS I–IV fördert:

- Die verschiedenen Arten von Leseverständnis: schnelles Lesen (skimming/scanning), detailgenaues Lesen (careful reading).

- Die Bewältigung längerer Texte unter Berücksichtigung verschiedenster Textsorten (Dialog, Artikel, Geschichte, Interview, Tagebucheintragung, Leserbrief, E-Mail etc.).

- Die Kompetenz im Umgang mit verschiedenen Testformaten (multiple choice, True/False-Entscheidungen, Ordnen, Einfüllen, Verstehen).

- Die Erschließung einfacher und schwieriger Vokabeln im Kontext durch gezielte Übungen (Einfüllen, Synonyme finden etc.).

- Angabe schwieriger Vokabeln im Text.

- Möglichkeit der Selbstkontrolle (Key).

www.ggverlag.at